simple
magic
tricks

hamlyn

simple magic

tricks

easy-to learn magic tricks with everyday objects

JON ALLEN

An Hachette UK Company
www.hachette.co.uk

First published in Great Britain in 2004 by
Hamlyn, a division of Octopus Publishing Group Ltd
Endeavour House
189 Shaftesbury Avenue
London
WC2H 8JY
www.octopusbooksusa.com

This edition published in 2013

Distributed in the US by
Hachette Book Group USA
237 Park Avenue
New York NY 10017 USA

Distributed in Canada by
Canadian Manda Group
165 Dufferin Street
Toronto, Ontario, Canada M6K 3H6

ISBN 978-0-600-62505-6

A CIP catalogue record for this book is available from
the British Library

Printed and bound in China

10 9 8 7 6 5 4 3 2 1

Contents

Introduction

Welcome to the amazing world of magic. This book contains 75 tricks, stunts and shows of skill that can be mastered by anyone, and which are all easy to do. They cover a wide range, from vanishes and appearances to predictions, animations, penetrations and more. While the methods are simple, the effects are pure magic; there are even some fancy flourishes. I include a number of these tricks in my own performances, which reflects how highly I rate them.

Because all the tricks in this book use everyday objects, many of them can be done on an impromptu basis – when someone asks you to do a trick, you can simply borrow a pack of cards, a coin, a pen, a piece of paper or whatever is to hand and do something magical. Some tricks require you to prepare something in advance, but in most cases

this is a one-time preparation. In other tricks, if you destroy the preparation, it is easy to either set up the trick or make the prop again.

You do not need to know any sleight of hand or difficult moves to perform any of the tricks in this book. While sleight of hand is required for more advanced magic, tricks performed well are often just as impressive to whoever is watching. As a professional magician, I know what the audience see is far more important than what's concealed from them. It is not always necessary to learn difficult or complicated routines to impress people. But even though the tricks here are simple, you need to practise to be able to do them smoothly and convincingly.

Learn to handle the props until you are comfortable with them. Repeat the actions as often as you need to for them

to become natural. Then, perform the trick in front of a mirror or, better still, try it out on a friend or family member. A mirror will show you what the audience will see, but you will be looking at your own reflection rather than at the person for whom you are doing the trick. So, practising in front of a real person is much more helpful.

Remember that an audience or helper will look wherever you look – to distract a person's attention from your hands, look directly at their face when you speak to them.

The secrets of magic are not in the props but in how you present them. When I see a trick I like or create a new one, I always ask myself how I can make it enjoyable for someone to watch. Simply performing the actions does not make a trick entertaining. I have given some tips and hints to help the presentation

and performance in many of the tricks. While they may not seem important, such subtleties make a difference to a trick's success. There are also a number of suggested variations, to help you think of different ways to perform some of the tricks.

Each trick is only as enjoyable as the performer finds it. My personality is different from yours, and yours is different from everyone else who reads this book. You make a trick unique by the way you perform it. Telling a story or having fun with the presentation makes people relax and enjoy the trick more. In my act, I like to use humour, and because my audience is enjoying watching me they don't worry about how the trick works. Do not copy other people's style, though; find one to suit you.

Practise, enjoy performing the tricks and have fun.

Always
Get it Right

THE ILLUSION

You place two packs of cards on the table, one of which contains a reversed card. This card will act as your prediction. A helper cuts the other pack anywhere they like, marking the place as they do so. You now open up the other pack and find the card you reversed earlier. This will match the card that your helper cut to.

This incredibly simple trick can be set up in a very short time. So, you will be able to impress your audience any time, any place, anywhere!

WHAT YOU NEED

Two packs of cards

DIFFICULTY
RATING: 1

1 Before you start, note the top card of one pack. This is the card that will be 'forced'. Find the same card in the other pack and reverse it in the middle of its pack.

2 To do the trick, get a helper to cut the first pack and place the upper portion to one side of the lower one. While the helper has a free choice to cut anywhere, ask them to cut the pack somewhere near the middle.

3 Pick up the lower portion and place it on top of the original top but at 90 degrees to it. The audience will believe that this is done to mark where the pack was cut.

4 Bring out the second pack of cards. Spread it out until you get to the reversed card in the middle. Point out that this card was reversed even before the helper cut the other pack.

5 Lift off the top portion of cards from the first pack and ask the helper to turn over the top card of the lower packet, which matches your prediction.

All Fingers
and Thumbs

THE ILLUSION

You create two piles, using a number of cards. After an extra single card is placed in one of the piles, it disappears and appears in the other pile.

Even though this is a self-working trick, your audience will be impressed. Each part of the trick involves a helper and seems to be honest and open, yet somehow you can still transfer the odd card from one pile to another. It will look impossible to your audience – yet of course it isn't.

WHAT YOU NEED

A pack of cards

DIFFICULTY RATING: 1

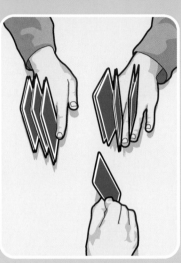

1 Ask a helper to rest their hands on the table. On one hand, place two cards between their fourth and their third fingers and say 'Two' out loud. Slip another two between the third and second fingers, two more between second and first, and another two between first finger and thumb. Each time say 'Two'. Repeat on the other hand, but place only a single card between the third and fourth fingers this time.

2 Take the first pair of cards and separate them into two piles, saying 'These two cards go here'. Take the next pair and place one on each pile, repeating the phrase each time. Continue with all the pairs in both hands until you reach the single card.

3 Ask your helper which of the two piles they would like the single card to be placed in. Whichever is selected, place the card in the middle of that pile. Now, square up both piles of cards.

4 Snap your fingers or wave your hands over each pile. Pick up the pile that you placed the single card in. Take the top two cards and drop them on the table, saying 'Two' out loud. Repeat with the next three pairs of cards, dropping them all into one pile. Make a big deal of the fact that the single card seems to have vanished.

5 Move to the other pile. Repeat the process of taking the top two cards, dropping them on to the table and saying 'Two'. After two more pairs of cards, you will find you are left holding a single card. Drop it on to the other cards, saying, 'And here's the odd card!'.

6 Be sure to count the cards off in pairs, rather than singly. Count two cards at a time, dropping each pair on to the table.

PRESENTATION

- *This is a mathematical trick where both the performance and the words that you say hide the method. By repeating a word or phrase each time a pair of cards is handled, the audience will become familiar with it. This detracts from the fact that you are separating the pairs of cards you made in the beginning, and making new pairs of cards at the end.*

- *You can make the trick more visual by placing a pen on the table before making the two piles. This acts as a 'wall' between the piles so you can't possibly sneak the card across.*

No Need to Guess

THE ILLUSION

While you are not looking, ask someone to choose a card from the pack and then replace it. Whichever card they choose, you will know which card was selected.

WHAT YOU NEED

A pack of cards

DIFFICULTY RATING: 1

PRESENTATION

• *The pack can be cut any number of times, and the chosen card will always be next to the 'key' card. But the pack must not be shuffled. Once you know the chosen card, you can enjoy revealing it in any number of ways.*

1 Get a helper to select a card from the pack. As the helper looks at the card and shows it to other people in the audience, secretly glimpse the bottom card of the pack and remember it – this card is your 'key' card.

2 Cut off the top half of the pack and place it on the table. Get the helper to place their card on top of the pile. Place the bottom half of the pack on to their card. This places the card you glimpsed right next to the chosen card.

3 While you do not know what the selected card is, you do know the card on top of it – your key card. When you spread out the cards and look through the pack, the card on the face of your key card is the one selected by your helper.

Clap the Deck

THE ILLUSION

A helper selects a card from the pack and replaces it while your eyes are shut. While they hold the pack, you knock out the other cards, leaving them holding their chosen card.

WHAT YOU NEED

A pack of cards

DIFFICULTY RATING: 2

PRESENTATION

• *If, when you hit the pack, no cards fall, ask the helper to loosen their grip a little and try again. If more than one card is left in the hand when you hit the pack, don't worry. Hit the remaining cards again. If only a few remain, pick all but the bottom one out and throw them down with the others. It will still be an impressive trick.*

1 Have a card selected and replaced next to a 'key' card as described opposite. Ask the helper to cut the pack several times. Hold up the pack so only you can see the faces and look through the cards as though trying to find the one chosen. Find your key card; the card in front of it will be the one they selected. Cut the pack so their card is on the bottom of the pack.

2 Ask the helper to hold their hand out, with palm uppermost. Place the pack face down on their fingertips and get the helper to place their thumb on top of the cards. Ask them not to hold the pack too tightly but not too loosely either, or the cards may fall out.

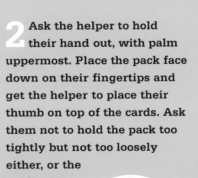

3 All you need to do now is hit the pack downwards near the short edge with your fingertips. (This does take practice!) All the cards will be knocked out the helper's hand...except for one card. Ask the helper to name their card, then turn over the card in their hand and watch their surprise as they see it is the one that they selected.

Feel the Pulse, Find the Card

THE ILLUSION

Someone chooses a card and replaces it within the pack without you seeing. Then, you pretend to use someone's pulse to help you find the card that they chose.

WHAT YOU NEED

A pack of cards

DIFFICULTY RATING: 1

PRESENTATION

• *To make this trick look as authentic as possible, really find the pulse. Get the helper to think of their card when they are pointing to it. You may feel the pulse jump as they are about to point to their card. Don't stop right at the card, but go past and then back to it, as though you felt something but weren't entirely sure.*

1 Get a helper to choose a card, then take it and replace it next to a 'key' card, as on page 12. The pack can be cut any number of times. Spread the cards face up in a straight line. You will see your key card and know the chosen card is the one on top of it.

2 Ask the helper who chose the card to hold out their hand and point the first finger. Place your fingers on their pulse. Find the pulse by placing two fingers lightly on the wrist at the bottom of the thumb. As they run their finger along the spread, pretend to feel a quickening in their pulse when they are hovering over their card. Call out 'Stop!' to show you felt the change and know which card is theirs.

Rising from the Deck

THE ILLUSION

This trick requires double magic! Not only are you able to guess correctly the chosen card but also you are able to make the card magically rise up out of the pack.

WHAT YOU NEED

A pack of cards

DIFFICULTY RATING: 2

PRESENTATION

- *Before the card is replaced, instruct the helper to rub it on their sleeve. Before you bring your index finger to the pack, rub it on your own sleeve as if you are creating a static charge. It will look as though the card is somehow 'sticking' to your finger by static electricity or some invisible force of attraction.*

1 Glimpse the bottom card (for your 'key' card, see page 12) as someone chooses a card from the pack. Replace this card next to your key card and ask the helper to cut the pack a number of times. Hold the pack so only you can see the cards and find your key card. The chosen card will be in front of it. Cut between them so the key card goes to the bottom and the chosen card goes on top.

2 Hold the pack in your left hand with all the cards, bevelled slightly upwards, facing the audience above the back of your hand. Bring your right hand from behind and extend your index finger so it rests on top of the pack. Behind the pack, extend your fourth finger so it touches the top card – the chosen one – with a little pressure. Raise your right hand straight up and the chosen card will stick to your fourth finger. It looks as though it is rising up and is somehow stuck to your extended index finger.

Und rcover C rd

THE ILLUSION
Although someone cuts the pack while it is under a handkerchief, you still know at what card the pack is cut.

WHAT YOU NEED
A pack of cards
A handkerchief or napkin

DIFFICULTY RATING: 3

PRESENTATION
• *This is an excellent trick where you know what card will be chosen before the trick starts. Practise turning over the cards with one hand under the handkerchief. Make sure that you have finished turning the cards over by the time they are visible. There should be no movement of the hand that is holding them.*

1 Before you start, look at the top card of the pack and remember it. Hold the pack face down in your right hand and drape the handkerchief over it with your left hand. As the pack goes out of sight to the audience, turn the pack face up under the handkerchief with your right hand. Make sure the pack does not show through the cloth.

2 Ask a helper to cut the pack through the fabric at any point. Demonstrate this if need be. As soon as the helper cuts the cards, turn the cards in your hand face down, keeping this action hidden by the handkerchief (see below). Then bring the cards out from underneath the handkerchief.

3 Hand the top card to your helper, who assumes this is the card to which they cut. Retrieve the handkerchief and cards from your helper and, as they look at their card, bring the bottom half of the cards back under the handkerchief, turn them face down and add them to the rest of the cards. Carefully turn the whole pack face down and bring them out into view. Finally, 'guess' the card your helper chose.

On Step Ahead of the Pack

THE ILLUSION

Each time you cut the pack you correctly guess the card that you have cut to. This trick will convince your audience that your first correct guess isn't just a fluke!

WHAT YOU NEED

A pack of cards

DIFFICULTY RATING: 1

PRESENTATION

• *You can repeat the cutting process any number of times, but no more than three or four is recommended. For the last one, get a helper to cut the cards and turn over the card that is cut to. Before naming the card, pretend to make a few mental calculations, as though this card will tell you the name of the next top card.*

1 Shuffle the pack into your right hand using an overhand shuffle. Make sure the faces of the cards are towards you. As you shuffle the cards, use your fingers to slightly push up the top card so you can glimpse it; now remember it. As soon as you have seen it, finish shuffling and place the cards face down on a table.

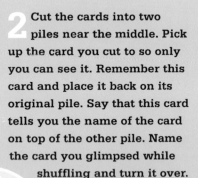

2 Cut the cards into two piles near the middle. Pick up the card you cut to so only you can see it. Remember this card and place it back on its original pile. Say that this card tells you the name of the card on top of the other pile. Name the card you glimpsed while shuffling and turn it over. Turn it back face down and place the other pile on top of it.

3 With the card you have just remembered on top of the pack, repeat the process by cutting the pack again. Look at the new card you have cut to, and remember it as before. Place it back face down and name the card on top of the other pile. This is the card previously cut to that you remembered.

Th Two--   d R v rs

THE ILLUSION

Two cards are chosen and replaced in the pack. Half the pack are face down in a face-up pack. But, when the pack is spread out, only two cards are face down – the chosen ones.

WHAT YOU NEED

A pack of cards

DIFFICULTY RATING: 3

PRESENTATION

- *When you make a secret move while shifting the audience's attention elsewhere, it is referred to by magicians as 'misdirection'. In this trick you are placing your card into the other person's packet of cards in order to encourage them to concentrate on something else and consequently you misdirect them.*

1 After shuffling the pack, cut it into two halves and ask a helper to choose which portion they would like. Get them to shuffle their cards while you shuffle yours. Make sure you finish shuffling your half before they do, look at and remember the bottom card, then secretly reverse it.

2 Ask the helper to spread through their cards, remove one and remember it. Do the same with your cards. Look at your card, but do not remember it – you must only remember the card you reversed beforehand.

3 Ask the helper to hold their cards out face down so you can replace your chosen card into their portion. Make sure nobody sees its face. While attention is on your card, secretly turn over the cards in your hand, hiding this action with your arm. The reversed card makes it look as though the cards are still face down – but only the top card is face down; all the cards underneath are face up.

4 Hold out your portion, making sure that no face-up cards are visible underneath the face-down top card. Ask the helper to push their card face down into your portion. As they squeeze their card in, make sure your cards remain squared together to avoid any face-up cards appearing and being seen.

5 Ask the helper to cut their portion in half and hand you the cut cards. Turn these cards face up and place them underneath yours, so that about half are showing. Turn the rest of the helper's cards face up and place them on top of your portion so about half of your cards are showing. Display the face-up and face-down groups, then square all the cards together.

6 Tell the helper you will try to turn all the cards up the same way except for the two chosen cards. Name the card you reversed at the beginning and get the helper to name their card. Spread the pack face up – two face-down cards will be visible. Turn them over to show that they are the cards you and your helper chose independently.

Do Exactly As I Do

THE ILLUSION

For this trick you'll need a helper. Each of you will take a pack of cards and will go through the same actions of shuffling the pack, then choosing and replacing a card. When you both present your chosen card, you will have miraculously picked the same one! This simple but impressive trick gives you practice of instructing a helper; it's also one used by many professional magicians.

WHAT YOU NEED

Two packs of cards preferably with different back designs or colours

DIFFICULTY RATING: 2

1 Give one pack of cards to your helper and keep the other for yourself. Each of you then shuffles your own pack. When you finish shuffling, glimpse the bottom card of your pack, which will be your 'key' card (see page 12). Place your pack slightly to the right in front of your helper and ask them to place their pack in front of you.

2 Cut off about two-thirds of your pack and place these cards to the left of the bottom third. The helper does the same. Now cut off half of the cards from the larger pile and place these to the left. Again, the helper follows your lead. This gives both of you three piles with roughly the same number of cards in each pile.

3 Take the top card of your middle pile and look at it. Get the helper to do the same and remember their card. Do not remember the one you take. Make sure no one except you can see the card you pick up. Place it back on top of the middle pile and instruct the helper to do the same with their card.

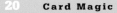

PRESENTATION

- *This is a simple but effective trick. At the end, before you reveal the two cards, remind the helper what has been done. Each pack was shuffled, the cards were cut randomly and a free choice of card was made. The card was then lost in the pack. By doing this, you make the helper remember what you want them to remember and forget other things, such as the swapping of the two packs.*

- *Emphasize how the person copied everything you did, and say how remarkable it is to go through all the random elements of the routine and end up with two identical cards.*

4 Pick up the pile on your right-hand side, which was the original bottom portion of the pack. Place these cards on top of the middle pile, then place this larger pile on top of the left-hand pile to leave one pile. The helper repeats this. By placing the original bottom portion on top of the middle pile, the helper has positioned your key card on top of their chosen card.

5 Swap the two packs so you hold the helper's pack and vice versa. Go through the cards, saying that you will find your card and they will find theirs. As you look through the cards, spot your key card. Their card will be the one in front of it. Place this card face down. The helper will find their card in your original pack and place it face down.

6 Explain how throughout the trick, the helper has copied all your actions. Go on to say that if everything has been done in exactly the same way, it follows that you should both have chosen the same card. Get the helper to turn over their card. Turn yours over – and watch their face when they see that they match.

Card Magic 21

Sort the Red from the Black

THE ILLUSION
A helper shuffles a pack of cards and you show them that the cards are mixed. But, after you deal the cards into two piles, the red and black cards have somehow separated.

WHAT YOU NEED
A pack of cards

DIFFICULTY RATING: 2

PRESENTATION
- *Just before you reveal the separated colours at the end, recall the process of the trick, emphasizing what you want the person to remember and helping them to forget you cut the cards.*
- *Watch carefully when your helper is shuffling. If they drop some cards or shuffle differently, the trick won't work, so be prepared to try again.*

1 Set up a pack of cards so the red and black cards alternate throughout the entire pack. Get a helper to mix the cards using a riffle shuffle; the easiest way to do this is to cut the pack into two halves then mix the cards by pushing them into each other. This action must be done only once; if it is repeated, the trick will not work.

2 Take the cards back from the helper and spread them out, showing how all the red and black cards are thoroughly mixed together. As you go through the cards, somewhere near the middle, find two cards together that are the same colour; the suits do not matter. Cut the pack between these two cards and complete the cut.

3 Deal the pack into two face-down piles. Make sure you keep the piles fairly neat and tidy, as you do not want any card moved out of position. Get the helper to choose a pile and pick it up while you pick up the other one. Deal the top card of your packet face up on to the table. Get the helper to deal their top card face down diagonally opposite the face-up card.

4 Deal your next card face up. If it is the same colour, deal it on to the first card; if it is a different colour, deal it next to the first card. The helper does the same, with their cards face down. Continue, with all the red cards going into one pile and all the black cards into another pile. There will be two piles, face down, opposite your face-up piles.

5 Turn over each of the face-down piles, putting them on to the face-up piles opposite them. The bottom card of the face-down pile should match the top card of the corresponding face-up pile.

6 Pick up the first pile and spread it out face up on the table to show that it contains only red cards. Do the same with the other pile to show it contains all the black cards. Despite all the shuffling and dealing, the colours have been separated.

Th Disappe ring Cut

THE ILLUSION

After threading a length of string through a straw, the idea is to cleanly cut the straw in two and show your audience the separate halves. The string is then magically restored. This trick looks really impressive; but your audience won't realize how easy it is to do. You will need to do a little preparation beforehand and practise handling the props. But it is well worth the effort.

WHAT YOU NEED

A length of string about
  30 cm (12 in)
A drinking straw
A pair of scissors

DIFFICULTY RATING: 3

1 First, prepare the straw: cut a lengthways slit in the middle of the straw about 4 cm (1½ in) long. If you use a straw with coloured stripes along its length, cut the slit where two colours meet, as this will help to conceal it.

2 To perform the trick, thread the string through the straw until the straw is in the middle of the length of string. About 10 cm (4 in) of string should hang out of each end of the straw. Hold the slit horizontally so the bottom of the straw faces down.

3 Hold the straw in both hands with your thumbs close together underneath and pressing slightly on the slit. Bend the straw in half, pushing your thumbs upwards and moving your hands downwards. Use your thumbs to make sure the slit does not widen and become noticeable.

4 While holding the bent straw in your left hand, take hold of both ends of the string with your right hand. Pull the ends downwards so that the string is forced down and out through the slit. Use the fingers of your left hand to hide the string that has come out of the straw.

5 Cut the straw with the scissors, making sure the scissors go above the string, which is visible to you alone. With the fingers of your left hand still hiding the string going across from one half to the other, show that the two halves of the straw are now separate pieces.

6 Take the straws in your right hand and hold them horizontally – grip one half at the base of your little finger and pivot the other half around, gripping it at the base of your thumb.

7 With your left hand, slowly pull one end of the string until it is completely removed from the straw. Then, hold it up to show that it is miraculously still in one piece.

'Armless Fun

THE ILLUSION
This simple trick will truly baffle your helper. As they watch a loop of string passes right through their arm.

WHAT YOU NEED
A length of string about 75 cm (30 in), tied into a loop

DIFFICULTY RATING: 2

PRESENTATION
• *Practise hooking your left finger into the right-hand loop until you can do it easily and without looking.*
• *Practise the timing of the last move so that the loop is pulled taut and both hands immediately move straight up. This improves the illusion.*

1 Ask a helper to hold out one arm. Place the loop underneath it and hold it taut between the second finger of each hand. Bring your hands up around each side of the arm so they nearly meet above it, then return them to their original position.

2 On the third or fourth time that you bring your hands up, secretly hook the loop held by the right hand with your left index finger.

3 As your hands go back down, let go of the loop with the left middle finger and pull the loop to the left with the left index finger.

4 Now, bring both hands straight up – it looks as if the string has passed right through the helper's arm.

Don't Lose Your Head

THE ILLUSION
A scarf, wound loosely about your neck, is then miraculously pulled through flesh and bone!

WHAT YOU NEED
A thin scarf, about 1.5 m (5 ft) long

DIFFICULTY RATING: 4

PRESENTATION
• *Make sure the loop created is hidden by your neck and is not visible from the side. Practise bringing it round behind your head as the left hand brings that end of the scarf up and around your head.*

1 Place the scarf around your neck so the left-hand end hangs lower down your front than the right-hand end. Grab the length on your left-hand side, about half-way down, with your right hand. Take hold of the right-hand length, near the end, with your left hand, making sure the longer length is behind your left arm.

2 Raise your right hand to bring the scarf up towards the right side of your neck. At the same time bringing the left hand straight up so that the longer length drapes over the shorter length, forming a loop.

3 Take the shorter length of scarf in your left hand up and around the right side of your neck so that it hangs down in front of your left shoulder. Let go of the loop in your right hand as you do so. The loop is now hidden behind your head. Take hold of each end and pull the scarf forwards. It will seem to your audience as if it has penetrated your neck.

Mysteriously Joined

THE ILLUSION

Two separate, looped lengths of rope are somehow joined together – this easy trick is impossible for the audience to work out. With the bottle as your cover, you are able to work your magic in the simplest and quickest way imaginable.

WHAT YOU NEED

Two pieces of rope
A coloured bottle with a
    large label

DIFFICULTY RATING: 4

1 Place the bottle on the table in front of you. Fold the two pieces of rope in half, holding each one near the top where the rope is looped. Hold both pieces of rope behind the bottle so that they are hidden from view.

2 Using the bottle as your cover, place the right-hand loop behind the left. Then, work the fingers and thumb on your right hand through the left-hand loop until they can fold it back and grip it. Do the same for the right-hand loop with your left hand, so each hand holds a loop folded back on itself. Now, the ropes are linked around each other in two places, one above and one below where you hold the loops.

PRESENTATION

- *Linking the two ropes is not difficult, but it must be done quickly and smoothly. You should practise so that you are able to make the link without looking, and at the same talking to the audience.*
- *As you bring the ropes up above the bottle, look at the loops yourself; if you look at them so will the audience. Don't rush this move, just smoothly and slowly bring the ropes forwards.*

3 As you bring the ropes up over the bottle, keep hold of the upper link while letting go of the lower link. Despite being released, the two ropes will still remain slightly twisted. Bring the other link forwards over the mouth of the bottle, and let the ropes hanging down drag along the bottle. As the ropes are brought forward, they untwist, with one going either side of the bottle.

4 The audience can see the two middles linked together but will not notice the ropes drag along either side of the bottle. They will believe that the ropes link behind the bottle.

The Eye of the Needle

THE ILLUSION

A piece of rope is wound around your thumb. Making a small loop with one end, you are able to magically thread the other end through the loop. To really impress your audience, you could even repeat the trick with your eyes closed. This is a quick illusion that can be done either as a magic trick or as a show of skill. Once you have mastered the method, it is something that can be done whenever and wherever you happen to be.

WHAT YOU NEED

A length of rope about 1 m (3 ft)

DIFFICULTY RATING: 2

1 Hold the rope in your right hand and position the base of your left thumb up against the rope about three-quarters of the way down its length. Let the shorter end of the rope hang over between the crotch of your thumb and your finger, while the longer side hangs nearest to you.

2 Wrap the longer end around your thumb by bringing it underneath your thumb then over the top towards you. Repeat until you have four or five loops wrapped around your thumb, just tight enough for the rope not to fall off.

3 Make a loop in the rope by bringing it up in front of your thumb and twisting it anticlockwise. Hold the loop with the fingers of the left hand so it sticks up above your thumb.

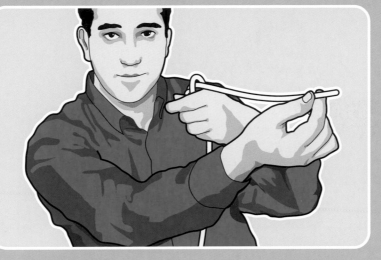

PRESENTATION

- *Act as though you are trying to thread a needle using the rope. As you pull the rope away from you, bring the right hand close to the loop so it looks as if the end went through the loop.*
- *To make this look more impressive, before winding the rope round your thumb, tie a big knot in the end of the short piece that hangs down. Make the loop smaller than the knot. This will add to the illusion that it is impossible for you to link the rope through.*

4 Take the other end of the rope with your right thumb and index finger, and hold it up with the end facing the loop. Your left fingers keep the hanging rope out the way. Relax the index finger of your left hand.

5 Quickly move your right hand, and its rope end, away from you. The rope appears to go through the loop in your left hand. If you pull the end back through the loop, you can repeat this as many times as you have loops around your thumb.

A Knotty Problem

THE ILLUSION

Ask anyone in your audience if they can tie a knot in a piece of rope without letting go of the ends and without folding their arms. When they admit defeat, you can show them how it can be done. This is a fairly well-known puzzle, but fools everyone who sees it every time.

WHAT YOU NEED

A length of rope about 1.5 m (5 ft)

DIFFICULTY RATING: 3

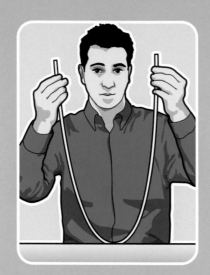

1 Hold the rope by the ends between your thumbs and first two fingers, with your hands at head height.

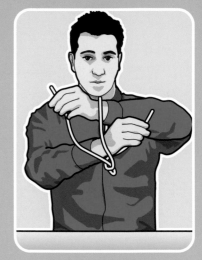

2 Keeping hold of the rope, move your right hand behind your left forearm, draping the rope over the left wrist, then back to the right. This part of the rope cuts across the piece hanging down underneath your left hand and creates two openings: a larger one underneath a smaller one.

3 Move your right hand back to the left and, from behind, take the rope into the lower, larger opening.

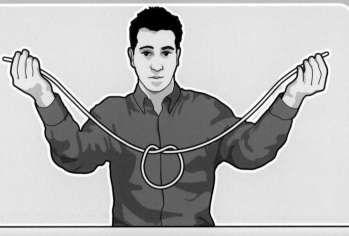

PRESENTATION
- *Each move should flow until the whole process is smooth.*
- *When you get to step 5, do not look at your hands. Try to focus on the middle of the rope, where the knot will appear. Remember, the audience's gaze will follow yours.*
- *As you make the knot, your right hand may need to re-grip further towards the end of the rope or your hand may be noticeably further down the rope. Secretly allow the right-hand end to slip down into your hand and grip the end again as you focus on the knot.*

4 Move your right hand backwards into the upper, smaller opening from the front, keeping your palm towards the audience. Pull your hands apart slightly, and the rope will be linked at a point near your right hand.

5 Keep pulling your hands apart to maintain a gentle tension on the rope. Rotate your right palm downwards so that it gets nearer the point where the rope links. Now, as the rope slips off your right wrist, let go of the end held by your right fingers, and take hold of the part of the loop that lay across your right palm.

6 Shake the rope off your left wrist and pull your hands apart to show everyone the knot in the middle of the rope.

The Coin Vanishes

THE ILLUSION

After a coin is wrapped inside a piece of paper, you rip up the paper and reveal that the coin has disappeared. This simple vanishing trick can be used again and again, using different objects whenever you need to make something disappear and then reappear in a different place. It is a good trick for practising hiding something in your hand while still holding it naturally.

WHAT YOU NEED

A coin
A square piece of paper, each side measuring just over three times the diameter of the coin

DIFFICULTY RATING: 3

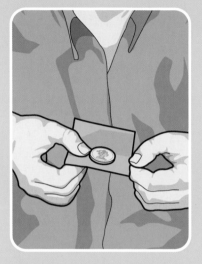

1 Place the coin on to the paper so it is slightly nearer the top edge than the bottom edge.

2 Fold the bottom edge up inwards and up towards the top edge, leaving a gap of about 1 cm (³⁄₈ in). You'll see that the coin now sits inside the paper on the fold.

3 Fold the left edge inwards and over to the right. Do not make the fold next to the coin but leave a slight gap.

PRESENTATION

- *As you make the folds, try not to look too much at your hands. You should be looking up and talking to your audience every so often, particularly as you make the last fold. When you have finished folding the paper, initiate eye contact with the audience as you allow the coin to slip gently into your hand.*

4 Do the same with the right edge, again leaving a gap between the fold and the coin. The coin should be able to slide a little inside the paper.

5 Turn the paper through 180 degrees so the last unfolded edges are now on the bottom, with the short edge facing you. Fold the exposed edge only away from you – do not fold both edges outwards. This leaves an opening at the bottom of the packet.

6 Hold the packet with your right hand underneath. Relax your grip and the loose coin will drop out on to the fingers of your right hand – curl them round it to hold it in place. Rip up the paper to show the coin has vanished.

Curr ncy Exch nge

THE ILLUSION

A coin is wrapped inside a piece of paper and when the packet is unwrapped, the coin has inexplicably changed into a completely different coin. Changing one object into another is a most magical thing. The best part of this trick is that you can change a small value coin into one of a larger value – something everyone would like to do!

WHAT YOU NEED

Two different coins
Two square sheets of paper the same size, about 20–30 cm (8–12 in)
A pair of scissors
Paper glue

DIFFICULTY RATING: 3

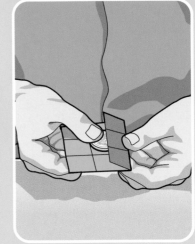

1 Fold a square sheet of paper into thirds horizontally and vertically so that you end up with nine identical squares, each one a little bit bigger than the largest coin. Repeat with the second sheet of paper.

2 Glue the back of the middle square of one sheet of paper to the back of the middle square of the second sheet so they line up perfectly. Let the glue dry, then place one coin in the middle of one sheet and fold it up around it.

3 To perform the trick, hold the sheets with the folded packet containing the coin underneath and the other sheet open on top. Place the other coin in the middle of the open sheet and fold this sheet around the coin.

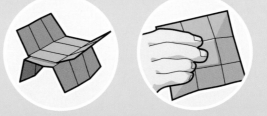

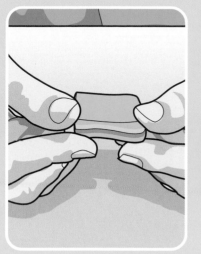

4 Hold the packet in the fingertips of your left hand with palm uppermost. Hold your right hand out palm up, turn your left hand palm down and place the packet in your right hand, thus turning the packet over. Curl your right fingers around the packet to conceal it.

5 Snap your left fingers over the packet. Open your right hand and unfold the top packet. The coin inside has changed.

PRESENTATION

- *Do not use card or thick paper: the thicker the paper you use, the bigger the hidden folded packet will be, and this will increase the chance of it being noticed. When cutting the two squares, make sure the edges are perfectly straight. The squarer the shape, the easier it will be to fold the packets to the same shape and size.*
- *Make sure the two packets line up exactly. If one overlaps the other, it will be seen by the audience. To help hide the packet underneath, show the top packet with the back edge slightly higher than the front edge so the whole packet is angled forwards.*
- *Try using other small, flat objects to vary the trick.*

Telekinetic Treasures

THE ILLUSION

After summoning up energy into your hand, sweep it towards a stood-up banknote and stop suddenly – the note promptly falls over.

WHAT YOU NEED

A banknote of any value or a rectangular piece of paper

DIFFICULTY RATING: 2

PRESENTATION

- *See how far away your hand can be so the note still falls over. About 15–17.5 cm (6–7 in) is good – but the further away, the better.*
- *To enhance the illusion, concentrate on the visual aspect of summoning up energy into your hand.*

1 Fold a banknote in half along its long edge. Stand the note upright on a table.

2 Stand or sit a short distance away from the note. Place your right hand over on your left side near your shoulder. Rub your hand on your sleeve as though building up static or some kind of invisible force.

3 With your palm facing sideways, swiftly swing it over so the fingers point to the note about 15 cm (6 in) away and stop suddenly. Just as your hand stops, open up your fingers as though sending out energy. The action of stopping suddenly causes the note to fall over because of the air current created.

Instant Print

1 Place a business card writing-side-down on your right fingers so the long edge nearest you is level with the base of your fingers.

2 Rotate your hand anticlockwise, at the same time closing your hand into a loose fist palm down around the card so the card turns over. Push the card out the side of your hand with your right thumb so the blank side is still showing. Pull the card out and repeat once or twice.

3 When ready to reveal the writing, place the card on the palm of your hand so the furthest long edge is level with the base of your fingers.

4 Bend your fingers round the card and turn your hand over. This time when your thumb pushes the card out, you can see the writing.

THE ILLUSION
Your personal details suddenly appear on a blank business card as you push it through your hand. This trick can be an effective – and memorable – way to hand out your business card to someone. The trick can be varied to suit the situation; it doesn't have to be a business card, you could write anything you like on a small card, even a proposal!

WHAT YOU NEED
A business card or other small card with writing on one side only

DIFFICULTY RATING: 2

Wish You Were Here...

THE ILLUSION
While the idea to pass your body through a postcard seems impossible, surprise your onlookers by proceeding to do exactly that.

WHAT YOU NEED
A postcard
A pair of scissors

DIFFICULTY RATING: 2

PRESENTATION
• *The thinner you make the strips, the bigger the loop will become. However, this also means that the loop becomes more fragile, so you must be careful not to tear it while climbing through.*

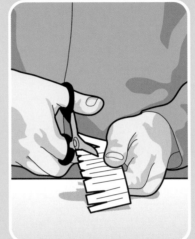

1 Fold the postcard in half lengthwise. Starting from the folded edge, make a cut about 0.5 cm (¼ in) from the short edge and stop when you are the same distance from the open edges. Turn the card around and make a cut 0.5 cm (¼ in) further in, stopping the same distance from the folded edge. Repeat all the way along the postcard.

2 Starting from the second strip in, trim off the folded edges, but stop short of the edge of the last strip. The first and last strips must still have folded edges.

3 Gently open up the postcard to show you have transformed it into a loop of card. Now you can carefully climb through this loop or pass it up and over your body.

S cr t Sque z

THE ILLUSION
Pick someone from the audience and show them a card with a hole in the middle. Ask them if they could push through a coin larger than the hole without tearing the card. Once they give up, you can show them how it is done. You will actually reveal the secret of this trick as you perform it, but it is fun to show a friend a quick, easy trick that they can then do themselves.

WHAT YOU NEED
A playing card or paper
A pair of scissors
A coin

DIFFICULTY RATING: 1

1 Before you start, cut a hole in the middle of a playing card slightly smaller than the coin. (An easy way to do this is to draw round a smaller coin then cut round the line.) Hold up the card and the larger coin, and ask a helper if they can push the coin through the hole without tearing or cutting the card.

2 When the helper has admitted defeat, fold the card in half. Place the coin in the middle of the card so that part of it shows through the hole. Hold the card by the bottom edges.

3 To push the coin through, move your hands upwards and inwards towards each other. This causes the two sides of the card to open out and the hole to widen slightly, allowing you to gently squeeze the coin through.

A Picture of Two Halves

THE ILLUSION

Having drawn a picture of a person on a strip of paper, you ask a helper to cut the strip anywhere they like. Afterwards when you reveal the two strips, you'll see that the cut has been made exactly in the middle of the picture, cutting the person in half. This trick allows you to concentrate on the presentation since the method is almost self-working and involves some canny misdirection.

WHAT YOU NEED

A thin strip of paper at least
   30 cm (12 in) long and
   5 cm (2 in) wide
A pencil
A pair of scissors

DIFFICULTY RATING: 3

1 On the top short edge of the strip of paper, draw the bottom half of a person.

2 On the bottom narrow edge of the strip, draw the top half of the person, making sure the lines at both edges meet when placed together.

3 Hold the strip in front by its top edge in your left hand, with the top half of the person on it facing you.

4 Ask a helper to go down the strip and cut straight across at any point they like. When they do this, allow the bottom section to drop to the floor or on to a table.

5 As you go to pick up the fallen piece, transfer the piece you are holding from your left hand to your right, turning it end for end as you do, thus moving the half picture on that piece from the top to the bottom.

6 Pick up the fallen strip and bring it to the bottom of the strip you hold so the two halves meet. It looks as if the helper has cut the woman cleanly in half.

PRESENTATION

- *When the strip falls to the floor, everyone will watch it fall. Keep your eyes on it as you go to pick it up. This is the point at which you switch the ends of the strip you hold.*
- *Having a picture of a person is one way to present this trick. As you do so, you can talk about the classic 'sawing a lady in half' illusion.*
- *You can have anything you like on the paper. What you draw will determine the presentation for the trick. For instance, you can get the helper to cut a picture of a piece of fruit or your name, with your first name above the cut and your surname below it. Try drawing or writing something that will make the trick unique to you.*

When is a Cut not a Cut?

THE ILLUSION

The preparation for this trick is well worth the effort, and even though you will be destroying the paper each time, it is easy to make more. This trick is not one for an impromptu show of skill, so save it for when someone asks to see a trick or you are doing a small show. Don't forget to try it out with paper money as well as normal paper – it works really effectively.

WHAT YOU NEED

A strip of paper at least
   25 cm (10 in) long and
   2.5 cm (1 in) wide
A pair of scissors
Talcum powder
Paper glue

DIFFICULTY RATING: 2

1 Lay the strip of paper down flat. Apply a thin layer of glue to the middle 2.5–4.0 cm (1–1½ in) of the strip. When it has dried, apply a thin layer of talcum powder to the glue so it is no longer tacky to touch.

2 When ready to perform the trick, take the scissors and cut the strip of paper in the middle. You will, of course, cut right through the area of glue.

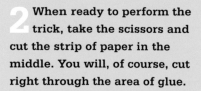

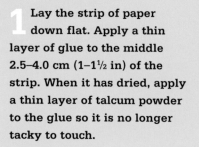

3 After you cut the paper, move your hands apart to show your audience that the paper really has been cut into two separate pieces.

4 Place the two halves together so that the glued areas are touching. Now cut a very thin piece off the end of the strip. As you do so, explain to your audience that, in order to restore the paper into one piece, you have to make a second cut.

5 Carefully open out the strip of paper – the two ends will have stuck back together from the pressure of the scissors during the second cut – and it will appear to be restored. You can casually waft it around, but put it away quickly as you don't want anyone to look too closely.

PRESENTATION

- *This trick works because when you cut through the glued area the first time, it exposes a thin edge of the glue. When the two halves are held together and cut through a second time, the scissors press the edges together, causing the two halves to stick to one another. This is why you must be careful when you open the strip out as the finale to your trick – if you wave it around too much, the two halves may fall apart.*

- *With practice, you will be able to work out exactly the amount of glue you need to apply and how much you can shake the strip of paper without the two halves coming apart.*

- *As a variation, why not try the same trick with two banknotes. Again, glue the middle section of each one and apply the talcum powder. Put the two notes face to face and cut them straight down the middle from top to bottom. You will have one half of each note in either hand. Place all four halves together and slightly bend one corner of each of the outer halves. Take the rear half in one hand and the outer half in the other. Quickly separate your hands and allow the two notes to unfold. What you actually have in each hand is one half of either note looking like a single note. Show them restored, then put them away quickly. Later, put each half back with its matching one.*

A Hard Act to Swallow

THE ILLUSION

This fun trick can be performed at any time while sitting at a table. You take a knife off the table and appear to swallow it. (Make sure you use a table knife not a knife with a sharp blade!) The advantage of such impromptu tricks is that you can perform them without having to carry any props around with you. Friends and members of your family will be impressed that you can turn a trick any time and anywhere.

WHAT YOU NEED

A table knife

DIFFICULTY RATING: 5

1 Sitting at a table, pick up the table knife in your right hand so the end is in the middle of your palm. Bring your left hand over so the tip of the blade is in the middle of your left palm. Hold your hands flat to the audience so that the knife is hidden from their view.

2 Raise your hands up to your mouth, turning them so the knife is vertical. The tip of the handle should be level with your mouth. Pause for a moment in this position. When you raise your hands to your mouth this first time, you are just teasing the audience.

3 Relax and bring your hands down, still holding the knife, on to the edge of the table. As you tell the audience that you are only teasing them, allow the knife to drop past the edge of the table on to your lap. Make sure that your hands do not move during this action.

PRESENTATION

PRESENTATION

- *Magicians rely a lot on moments when the audience is relaxed as their concentration levels decline. There is tension as they watch you raise the knife the first time, but when you drop your hands to the table and make a few comments, they relax. This is the moment to drop the knife.*
- *The second time your hands go up, they must look exactly the same as when the knife was there. Practise keeping the hands in the same position.*

4 Now explain to your audience that this time you will really eat the knife and raise your hands up to your mouth again, exactly as you did before. This time bring your hands downwards, as though the knife was going into your mouth.

5 At the point where the end of the knife would have been going past your mouth, pretend to swallow. Open your mouth to show that it is empty and open out both hands to reveal the fact that the knife has disappeared.

Mark My Hands

THE ILLUSION
A black mark on the palm of your hand magically vanishes and appears on the hand of a helper. Magic tricks that involve other people are always powerful. This is one of the best, as not only are you showing the helper a good trick, but they become one of the props. It is also another example of a trick that can be performed on an impromptu basis.

WHAT YOU NEED
A felt-tip pen (black works best)

DIFFICULTY RATING: 4

1 Just before you start, secretly draw a black mark on the tip of the middle finger of your right hand. You may need to apply it a few times to ensure you have a good supply of wet ink on that finger.

2 Ask a helper to hold out both their hands palm down. As you ask them to hold their hands a little higher, take both hands and gently press upwards into their palms with your fingers. This transfers the mark to their left palm. This action must seem natural or it is likely to be noticed and remembered.

3 Get the helper to drop their right hand and make their left one into a fist. Take out the pen and draw a mark on the palm of your left hand. Do not make it as bold as you did with the one previously drawn on your fingertip.

4 Use the first two fingers of your right hand to rub out the mark on your palm. The ink will vanish from your palm and from your right fingertip as well.

5 Show that the mark on your palm has vanished. Ask the helper to open their fist and show that the mark has now appeared on their palm.

PRESENTATION

- *Don't grab the helper but gently raise their hands a little higher or further apart. Otherwise you could position them by gently leading them by the hand. The action of taking the hand will go unnoticed.*
- *Maintain eye contact and talk to the helper as you draw the mark on their hand. Avert your gaze from your hand; you don't want to draw attention to this area.*
- *Take your time and don't rush. The longer the time taken between placing the mark and revealing it at the end, the more likely it is that the helper will forget you touched their hand.*

The Jumping Ring

THE ILLUSION

A ring jumps from one finger to another, then back again, all in the blink of an eye. This very visual trick takes people by surprise. It is a good idea to borrow a ring from the person who is helping you to increase the plausibility of your performance – your helper won't be able to fathom where on earth you could have got an identical ring.

WHAT YOU NEED

A finger ring

DIFFICULTY RATING: 2

1 Place the ring on your right middle finger. Place your first and second fingers in a 'V' shape on the back of your left arm.

2 Raise your right hand off your arm about 15 cm (6 in). As you do so, quickly curl in your index finger and straighten out your third finger.

3 Bring your hand back down to where it started. It will look like the ring has switched fingers. Raise your right hand off your arm again. This time, curl in your third finger and straighten out your index finger. Bring your hand down and the ring seems to have jumped back to the finger from where it started.

A Peculiar Pencil

THE ILLUSION
You pick up a pencil and place it on the palm of your hand, where it appears to stick without any means of support. Pens work equally well. As pens and pencils are objects people often carry around with them, you have the opportunity to perform this trick anywhere.

WHAT YOU NEED
Two pencils
A watch or rubber bands
Long-sleeved top

DIFFICULTY RATING: 2

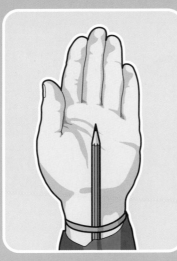

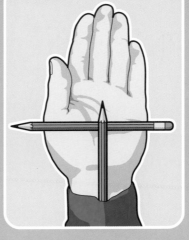

1 Before you start, place one pencil on the inside of your left wrist under your watch (or rubber bands) so that the end extends to the middle of your left palm. Keep the watch or bands hidden beneath your sleeve.

2 Take the other pencil and, with the back of your left hand towards the audience, place it between your palm and the pencil. By pressing your palm against the first pencil, the second one will appear to stick to your palm.

PRESENTATION
- *You can pretend to hold the pencil in place by grabbing your left wrist and extending your right index finger. People will see only three fingers and assume you are holding the pencil in place with your hidden finger.*
- *If you are careful, you can get several pencils and appear to have them all stick to your hand. By not calling attention to how many there are, when you take them away, you can also take away the one under your watch. This is very helpful in getting rid of the evidence!*

Mysterious Movements

THE ILLUSION

Use your magic – in this case careful and surreptitious blows – to make a straw roll around all on its own.

WHAT YOU NEED

A drinking straw

DIFFICULTY RATING: 2

PRESENTATION

• *To add some drama, move your finger around the straw as though making a circle of energy around it. Do not make it obvious that you are blowing downwards, and don't puff out your cheeks or purse your lips – as these are obvious tell-tale signs!*

1 Place the straw on a table so the long edge is about 15 cm (6 in) away from the edge of the table. Place your right index finger slightly to the right of the straw.

2 Blow at a spot just to the left of the straw, and watch as it starts to roll away to the right. Then, move your hand to the right and the straw will appear to follow it.

3 Instead of using your finger, you could also place your hand above the straw. As long as you can still blow on to a spot near the left-hand side, the straw will still move.

From Out of Nowhere

THE ILLUSION

As you snap your fingers, a handkerchief appears in your hand. This trick does need to be set up in advance so you must be ready beforehand. Some of the other tricks in this book require a handkerchief as a prop – so what better way of introducing it than having it appear from nowhere?

WHAT YOU NEED

A handkerchief
A long-sleeved top

DIFFICULTY RATING: 2

1 Before you start, hold the handkerchief by a corner and wrap it quite tightly around your index finger.

2 When you have finished, place the wrapped handkerchief in the crook of your elbow. Bend your arm so that the handkerchief is hidden from view. Make sure you can still move your arm quite naturally while it's bent.

3 Depending on which elbow is hiding the handkerchief, snap the fingers of the same hand as you quickly straighten out your arm. Watch as the handkerchief shoots forwards and opens out. Catch it in the same hand, and it will appear to have come from nowhere.

THE ILLUSION

This is another example of a trick that can be performed impromptu and with borrowed items. If you use a napkin while at a friend's house, you will definitely grab their attention as you push the knife through it! Create an impressive routine by performing this trick with others in this book that use the same props.

WHAT YOU NEED

A table knife
A napkin or handkerchief

DIFFICULTY RATING: 5

1 Hold the knife high up on the handle in your right hand. Place the napkin just below the centre of the knife and then drape it over the top so one corner rests on your arm and the corner diagonally opposite hangs down in front.

2 As you smooth the napkin, hold a small piece of the material with your left thumb. Lift the front corner back over the knife to show it is still there. Clip the corner draped on your arm with the fingers and thumb of your left hand.

3 Pick up this corner as you bring your left hand forwards and over the knife, covering it again. This time, both corners are in front of the knife. Use your right thumb to clip a small piece of material folded around the knife tip.

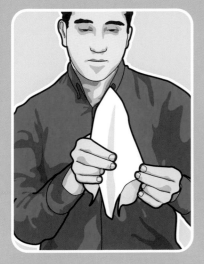

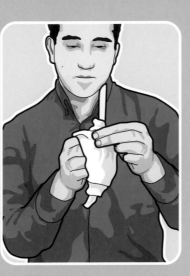

4 With your left hand, pull the folded piece down tightly against the knife. Now release the material with your right thumb and smooth the napkin around the knife.

5 Work the napkin between your hands so the tip of the knife loosens from beneath the fold. Push the knife up from below until it appears from behind the napkin. From the front, it appears to have penetrated the fabric.

6 Continue to work the knife upwards until it completely clears the napkin. Hold the knife in your right hand and open out the napkin. The knife went right through it – but there is no hole in the napkin whatsoever!

Cutlery Transformations

THE ILLUSION

A fork is wrapped inside a napkin. When the napkin is unwrapped, the fork has mysteriously transformed into a knife. You can perform this trick on the spur of the moment. By pretending not to have a knife but to have an extra fork, you have created a reason for changing the fork into a knife. Giving the audience a reason for performing magic always makes the trick more remarkable.

WHAT YOU NEED

A napkin
A table knife
A fork

DIFFICULTY RATING: 4

1 Place the knife on the table sideways on to you. Place the middle of a flat napkin over the knife so one corner is nearest you. Make sure the shape of the knife is not seen and the knife is not visible. Place the fork on the napkin to the side of the knife nearest to you, again sideways on to you.

2 Pick up the corner of the napkin nearest to you and fold it over to the opposite corner. Position it so that it doesn't quite reach the corner but stops just short of it.

3 Using both hands, with the fingers on top and thumbs underneath, pick up the knife and fork through the napkin. Wrap the knife and fork inside the napkin by rolling it around them towards you.

- Make sure the napkin is not too flat or the knife's outline will show. Also make sure the napkin is thick enough to hide the knife completely.

- To get rid of the fork at the end of the trick, gather up the napkin and drag it across the table towards you. The fork will fall off the edge of the table and land in your lap. Be careful and don't let it make any noise.

4 Roll the napkin until the shorter corner rolls around and underneath. It should pop out from underneath, leaving the longer corner on your side and the shorter corner on the far side of the wrapped cutlery.

5 The napkin has now turned over. Take hold of the two corners and gently pull the nearest one towards you while pulling the furthest one away from you.

6 When the napkin has unfolded, the knife now appears on top; the fork lies hidden underneath. The transformation is complete.

The Glass Vanishes

THE ILLUSION

You cover a glass with a napkin. After placing it in the middle of the table, you bring your hand down on to the napkin, only for the glass to vanish. Professional magicians have been performing this trick over many years and it is considered a classic and always provokes a strong reaction from the audience. Timing and misdirection are important aspects of this routine so make sure you practise until all the moves are seamless.

WHAT YOU NEED

A napkin
A tumbler glass

DIFFICULTY
RATING: 4

1 Place the glass on the table; the glass must be a tumbler style without a stem. Place the middle of the napkin over the glass.

2 Smooth the napkin down the sides of the glass so it is a tight fit. The outline of the glass should be visible.

3 Pick up the napkin with the glass underneath and bring it back to the edge of the table. At the same time, bring attention to the spot it was picked up from by pointing to it and talking about it. As everyone looks at where you are pointing, allow the glass to slip out from under the napkin and drop into your lap.

4 Bring the napkin back to the spot you pointed to. The napkin holds the shape of the glass, making it appear as though the glass is still underneath it.

5 Pause for a moment, then bring your free hand up above the napkin. Pause again to heighten the tension.

6 Bring your hand down quickly, flattening the napkin. The glass has vanished. You can leave it vanished or produce it from under the table as though you have pushed it through.

A Balancing Act

THE ILLUSION

You place a wine glass on the edge of a plate held vertically, where it remains balanced.

WHAT YOU NEED

A plate
A wine glass

DIFFICULTY RATING: 3

PRESENTATION

• *Keep your thumb in position at all times, rather than moving it into position on the third try. This eliminates any movement of your right hand at the last moment. If you look as though you really are trying to balance the wine glass, the trick will be more believable. Don't leave the glass for too long – a couple of seconds is enough.*

1 With your right thumb underneath and fingers on top, pick up a clean plate and hold it vertically, with the base of the plate facing away from you. Your hand should be holding the plate at the two o'clock position. Your thumb should be able to reach just below the top edge of the plate.

2 Gently place the wine glass on top of the edge of the plate. Take it off, then place it back on, as though you are trying to find its balancing point. On the third attempt, place the glass slightly off-centre towards you.

3 With your thumb extended, you can hold the glass steady on the tip of your thumb and the plate. From the front, it looks as if the glass is balanced on the edge of the plate. Leave it for a few seconds, then lift it off and place it back on the table.

Twist or Stick?

THE ILLUSION
You wrap two straws around each other, twisting them together, yet you can still pull them apart. As you appear to twist the straws more and more tightly, it will create the effect of being impossible to separate them.

WHAT YOU NEED
Two drinking straws

DIFFICULTY RATING: 2

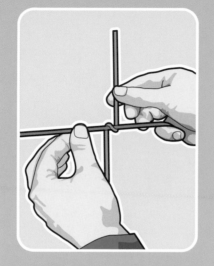

1 Hold a straw in each hand; grasp the left-hand straw horizontally and the right-hand one vertically behind it, with the middles touching. Wrap the top of the vertical straw towards you around the horizontal and back to the top.

2 Holding the middles in place, wrap the right end of the horizontal straw towards yourself and around the vertical straw back to the right-hand side. Press the middles gently together to hold them in position.

3 Bring the left end over to the right and hold them both in your right hand. Take hold of the top and bottom ends in your left hand. Now, pull both hands apart – the straws will appear to pop through each other.

Will it Burst?
Part 1

THE ILLUSION

You blow up a balloon then push a needle all the way through without it popping. This is one of the most visually striking tricks in the book and will have your audience holding their breath in anticipation. Practise until you feel confident of completing the trick first time every time; it's a good idea to have some spare balloons to hand, though, just in case!

WHAT YOU NEED

A balloon
A long thin needle

DIFFICULTY RATING: 3

1 Blow up the balloon to about half its full size and tie off the neck. There should be an uninflated area near the neck and at the base opposite it. Dip the needle in some water so it is damp, then place the tip very near the neck in the uninflated area.

2 Gently push the needle into the balloon; be assured, it will not burst. Continue to push the needle in towards the end, making sure the tip presses against a portion of the uninflated area on the balloon's end.

3 Carry on pushing the needle through until it comes out through the end. Show the audience that the needle has gone all the way through the balloon. After giving everyone a good view, pull the needle out. The balloon will now let out air, so pop it as the finale.

Will it Burst?
Part 2

THE ILLUSION
It is best to perform this trick at a distance from your audience so that the sticky tape isn't obvious.

WHAT YOU NEED
A balloon
A long thin needle
Clear sticky tape

DIFFICULTY RATING: 3

PRESENTATION
• Hold the balloon so the tape is just out of view of the audience, who must be able to tell that the needle is going into the balloon. You can gently push it against the opposite side, but don't do this too hard.

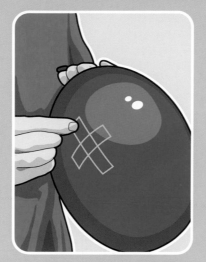

1 Before you start, blow up the balloon to nearly full size and tie off the neck. Place a small 'X' of clear sticky tape on the side of the balloon.

2 When you are ready to perform the trick, hold the balloon with the tape towards you. Push the needle through the middle of the 'X' into the balloon. If the needle goes through the tape, the balloon will not burst.

3 Take the needle out of the balloon and cover the hole with your thumb to stop the balloon deflating. If you put more tape in another spot (on the same side of the balloon) you could repeat the trick. To finish, simply pop the balloon with the needle.

Band on the Run

THE ILLUSION

A rubber band jumps from one set of fingers to another. This widely known trick is one of the oldest in the magicians' circle. Its simplicity makes it a great linking trick in a routine, and with just a rubber band as a prop, it can be performed anywhere and at any time.

WHAT YOU NEED

A rubber band

DIFFICULTY RATING: 2

1 Place the rubber band around the index and middle fingers of your right hand. You want it to be tight enough to cling to the fingers but not too tight.

2 Stretch the band a few times. The last time you stretch the band, close your fingers into a fist, making sure all your fingers slip inside the band.

3 Hold your hand in a fist facing outwards, with the palm of your hand and fingers facing towards you.

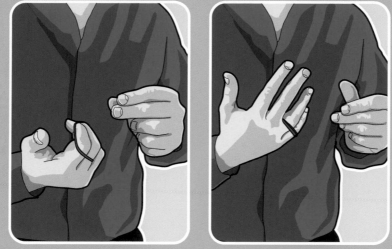

PRESENTATION

• *You can use any width of rubber band for this trick. The best way to get the right tension is to put a rubber band on your two fingers. If it is too loose, wrap it around the fingers until it is just tight enough not to fall.*

4 Quickly straighten your fingers. The band will jump from your first two fingers to the last two fingers. If you are quick enough, give your fist a quick shake as you open and close your fingers so the magic happens in a blur and your hand remains in a fist.

5 Try to give your tricks a 'magical moment' – a snap of the fingers, a wave of the hand or a 'Three, two, one' count. This moment suggests to the audience the moment the magic happens. Here, snapping the fingers of your left hand towards your fist as the band jumps across enhances the performance.

Jumping Bands

THE ILLUSION

Two different-coloured rubber bands jump between your fingers and switch places. A good way to present this trick is to perform Band on the Run (see page 64) first and then follow it with this trick. While the actions of this version are the same, the process of the bands switching places will appear to be more difficult to your audience.

WHAT YOU NEED

Two different-coloured rubber bands

DIFFICULTY RATING: 2

1 Place one rubber band around your first and second fingers, and the other one around your third and fourth fingers. Pull down on both bands. Move one band over the other so you have an overlapping section. Bend all four fingers so the tips go into this intersection.

2 All this is hidden from the audience's view and should look as if you are just stretching the bands and bending your fingers into a fist. From the front, you still have the rubber bands on separate pairs of fingers.

3 Straighten out your fingers, and the two bands will automatically jump across to switch fingers.

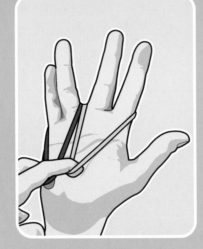

Trading Places

THE ILLUSION

In a similar vein to Jumping Bands (opposite), this trick involves two rubber bands switching places. However, here you have one rubber band looped around your finger, with another hanging from it. In this very quick trick the bands change places in an instant. Use two different-coloured bands to enhance this trick. Take the time to practise so that you can perform the moves smoothly and without hesitation.

WHAT YOU NEED

Two different-coloured rubber bands

DIFFICULTY RATING: 2

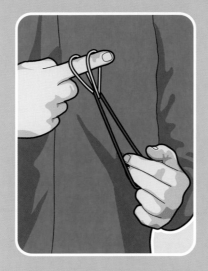

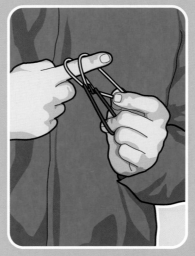

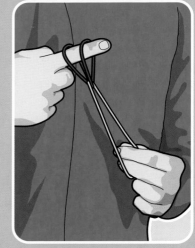

1 Thread one rubber band through the other and double it over itself. Hang this folded band over your right index finger so the other band hangs down underneath. Pull down on the other band using the thumb and the first two fingers of your left hand to show the bands are linked.

2 Pull down two or three times, then just before you pull down again, let go with your left index finger and grip part of the folded band.

3 Keep your index finger grip and simultaneously release the second finger's hold on the other band. Pull down with your index finger, and the two bands can be seen to have changed places.

Op n Sesam !

THE ILLUSION

Two closed safety pins open themselves in your hand. Although this trick does need to be set up beforehand, it is almost self-working. But, this doesn't mean you don't have to work at it! Like all the tricks in this book, make sure you practise first before you show people. The subtle difference between a polished trick and a slightly fumbled one can make all the difference.

WHAT YOU NEED

Two large, identical safety pins

DIFFICULTY RATING: 2

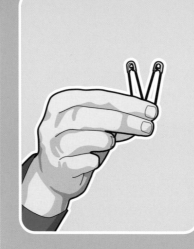

1 Before you start, open both safety pins. Place them together with the sharp point of each pin held in place by the other pin's safety guard. Hold them as near to the base as possible to cover where they cross – from the front it should look as if both pins are normal and closed.

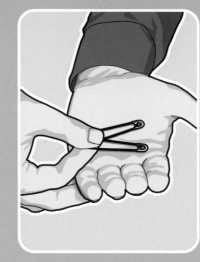

2 Place the pins on the palm of your hand and curl your fingers around them. Just as the pins go out of sight of the audience, let go of them. Turn the top one around so both pins face the same direction. Close your hand into a fist.

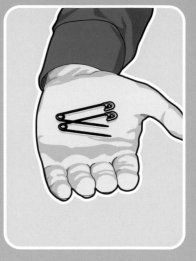

3 Make a magical gesture over your closed fist and open it. The pins have somehow managed to open themselves. Very gently drop the pins on to the table or into someone's hand. You will leave your audience clueless.

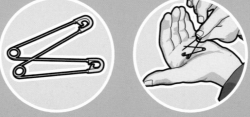

Unlock the Pins' Secret

THE ILLUSION
Two safety pins are locked together, yet can be pulled apart with just one gentle tug. This trick is best shown as one of a series: start to create a routine by linking it to other tricks using the same props.

WHAT YOU NEED
Two large, identical safety pins

DIFFICULTY RATING: 3

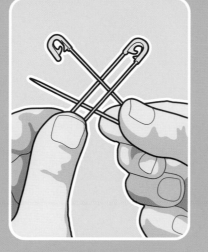

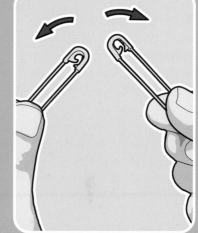

1 Open one of the pins and link it through the other one. It is important that the opening bar of the pin in your right hand is to the right and the opening bar of the pin in your left hand is on the bottom. Grasp both pins firmly by their bases.

2 Holding the pins at an angle to form an 'X', apply gentle pressure on the pins by twisting your right hand slightly away from you while twisting your left hand slightly towards you.

3 Pull both hands apart sharply, and the pins will come apart without opening. This is something that takes practice, but once you get the knack it becomes much easier.

Watch it Go!

THE ILLUSION

A pin is secured to a handkerchief but is then miraculously moved to another point while it remains secured. This trick is clever even when you know the secret and once you are confident about performing it, you can even ask to borrow a handkerchief or a shirt from someone in the audience – this would really make people hold their breath!

WHAT YOU NEED

A large safety pin
A handkerchief

DIFFICULTY RATING: 4

1 Get a helper to hold the handkerchief in front of them. It must be held by the top corners and stretched taut.

2 Push the pin through the handkerchief very near the top edge and to the left of the centre as you look at it.

3 Close up the pin, securing it on the handkerchief. Make sure you hold the pin firmly in your right hand with the opening bar on the right and the pin angled to the left.

PRESENTATION

- *This trick looks amazing but is very simple once you get the knack. Try it out on an old handkerchief first, as it may rip a little on the first few attempts.*
- *Be sure to keep pulling down slightly as you slide the pin across. This helps to keep the pin from sliding off the top of the handkerchief.*
- *Once you get the hang of this trick and can slide the pin quickly and smoothly, you may feel confident enough to try it without covering the pin. This looks even more incredible.*

4 Place your left hand in front of the pin to hide it from view. Once hidden, pull the pin down so the material enters the guard. While maintaining a slight downward pressure, sharply pull the pin to the right. The pin comes free from the handkerchief and rides along it. Keep it hidden with your left hand.

5 After sliding the pin for about 15–20 cm (6–8 in), push the pin back into the handkerchief. Now you can move your left hand away to show the pin is still secured and through the handkerchief.

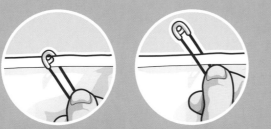

The Mint with the Hole

THE ILLUSION

A mint is threaded on to a piece of string. With the ends of the string held by a helper, you cover the mint with a handkerchief. You then reach underneath and remove the unbroken mint from the string. This trick requires a little more practice than most so invest your time wisely.

WHAT YOU NEED

Two mints with holes in the middle

A length of string 50–61 cm (20–24 in)

A handkerchief

DIFFICULTY RATING: 4

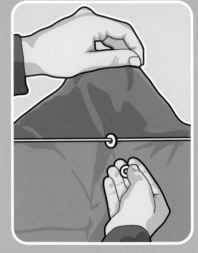

1 Before you start, carefully break one of the mints in half. Slightly moisten the exposed areas, then press the two halves back together until they stick. Hide a second mint in your right hand by holding it at the base of your fingers, curling them slightly around it to keep it hidden.

2 When you are ready to do the trick, thread the broken mint on to the string. The audience should not be aware of the second mint you are holding in your hand. Ask a helper to hold on to each end of the string, keeping it taut.

3 As you cover the mint with the handkerchief, hold the second mint at your fingertips – but not until your hand is hidden from the audience. Let the handkerchief hang on the string.

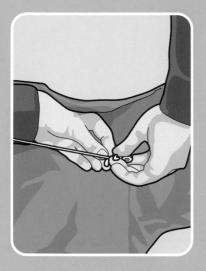

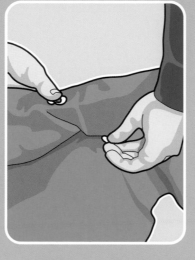

PRESENTATION
- *When you hide the mint in your hand, look natural. Don't grip the mint, but simply let it stay in place. You can still move your fingers, so don't worry about it. The audience does not know it is there, so concentrate on the other props and nobody will guess you are hiding anything.*
- *When you have removed the handkerchief, put it in your pocket. You can take it out again later, leaving the broken pieces of mint in the pocket.*

4 Under cover of the handkerchief, carefully break the mint on the string. It will come apart easily, as it is already broken. Make sure you do not drop either of the broken pieces.

5 Take both broken pieces in your left hand and grab hold of the handkerchief as well. Move the second mint to a point where the broken one was on the string.

6 Remove the handkerchief to show the mint has been magically removed from the string without breaking it.

Through the Drinking Glass

THE ILLUSION

You stuff one handkerchief inside a glass. Despite the handkerchief being trapped, you are somehow able to pull it through the base of the glass. This penetration trick is both simple and startling. While the audience will be convinced by what you are doing, you are setting up the trick right under their noses. With careful practice, you will find that you can get away with some very bold moves.

WHAT YOU NEED

Two handkerchiefs
A glass
A rubber band

DIFFICULTY RATING: 3

1 The glass must be a tumbler style with straight sides. Stuff one of the handkerchiefs all the way into the glass, making sure a corner is easily accessible. Hold the glass by the sides, with your hand underneath.

2 Place the other handkerchief over the glass. As soon as the glass is hidden from the front, loosen your grip and allow the glass to pivot upside down. Make sure the handkerchief in the glass does not fall out.

3 Place the rubber band around the glass and the handkerchief. The audience assumes the glass is still mouth upwards.

- *When pivoting the glass at the beginning and end of the trick, don't make any tell-tale movements with your hand. Remember that you are not supposed to be doing anything in these moments.*
- *Pull the handkerchief out from the side and not from the bottom of the glass. This makes it seem more impossible and stops people thinking the glass is somehow upside down.*
- *Practise until you can do all the secret moves smoothly without any hesitation.*

4 Reach under the handkerchief and grab the accessible corner of the handkerchief in the glass. Pull it out sideways as though you are pulling it through the side of the glass. Keep pulling until the handkerchief is completely free and let it fall into your lap out of sight.

5 Reach under the handkerchief covering the glass and, again, hold it loosely by the sides with your hand underneath. Remove the handkerchief covering the glass and when the rubber band pops off, pivot the glass back the right way round. Lift the handkerchief all the way off to show the glass is empty and the right way up.

Where Did the Money Go?

THE ILLUSION

You drop a coin into a glass, where it instantly vanishes. This is a great trick to do on the spur of the moment. The puzzling part is that the coin is heard to drop into the glass yet still disappears without trace. It shows how people are fooled not just by what they see but also by what they hear. Magicians use all the senses to fool an audience.

WHAT YOU NEED

A coin
A glass
A handkerchief

DIFFICULTY RATING: 3

1 Drape the handkerchief over your left hand. Place the coin so it is gripped by your left fingers through the centre of the handkerchief.

2 Tip the glass slightly towards the coin. Turn your left palm down so the coin is held over the mouth of the glass. Tip the glass back so it is upright.

3 Cover the glass with the handkerchief, with the coin still over its mouth. The audience should be able to see the outline of the coin and the glass through the fabric.

4 Lift the coin upwards slightly, as though repositioning the handkerchief. Then shake it forwards and backwards a little. At the same time, tilt the glass forwards so the coin is now positioned over the side of the glass.

5 Let go of the coin. It will drop and a noise will be heard as it hits the glass. It will sound like it has hit the bottom of the glass, but it has actually hit the side and landed in your hand.

6 Pick up the covered glass in your right hand and place it in front of you on the table. Move your right hand back to the edge of the table and allow the coin to drop gently into your lap.

7 Make a magical gesture above the glass and lift off the handkerchief. The coin has somehow vanished from inside the glass.

Alphabetical
Assistance

THE ILLUSION

Without you seeing, someone selects a coin from those that are on the table. You instantly know which coin is chosen. In this simple mathematical trick you can concentrate on a good presentation to make it fun and magical. While the trick is described here with coins, you can use any type of small objects. This makes it a very good impromptu trick.

WHAT YOU NEED

15–20 assorted coins

DIFFICULTY RATING: 1

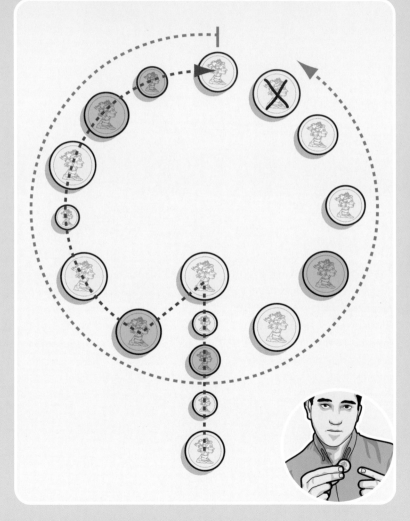

1 Place five coins in a line on the table. Place the other coins in a circle so the shape looks like a letter 'Q' with a long tail.

2 Get a helper to think of a number between 10 and 20. Starting at the tip of the tail, ask them to count up then go clockwise around the circle to their number. Starting with the coin arrived at, they then count the same number again anticlockwise, missing out the tail and carrying on round the circle. They remember the coin they finally land on.

3 All this is done while your back is turned. You know which coin will be arrived at by counting the coins in the tail. Their coin will be this many to the right of the tail; it doesn't matter what number they choose. Pretend to concentrate, then pick up the right coin.

C n You Fe l the Heat?

THE ILLUSION

A helper chooses a coin, marks it and drops it back with the others. You pick out the marked coin first time.

WHAT YOU NEED

A selection of coins
A marker pen
An opaque glass or container

DIFFICULTY RATING: 2

PRESENTATION

- *If possible, cool down the coins before you start. This makes the difference in temperature between the marked coin and the others more noticeable.*

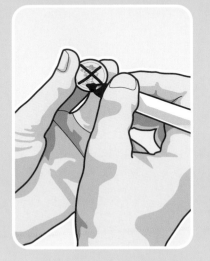

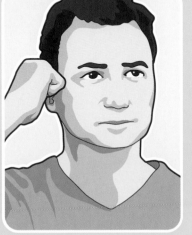

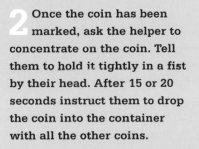

1 Put a selection of different coins in the container and ask a helper to choose one. Turn your back and tell them to put a mark on the coin so they can identify it later.

2 Once the coin has been marked, ask the helper to concentrate on the coin. Tell them to hold it tightly in a fist by their head. After 15 or 20 seconds instruct them to drop the coin into the container with all the other coins.

3 Turn halfway to the container and without looking, reach in and remove one coin at a time, eventually removing the marked coin. The coin that was held tightly will be warmer than the others. When you feel a coin is slightly warmer than the others, you know it is the marked one.

A Disappearing Act

THE ILLUSION

A coin vanishes as it is placed in your hand then reappears from nowhere in your helper's hand. This wonderful trick also offers a good lesson in making someone concentrate on something they think is important – misdirection. When you can master this, you can do many great magic tricks. In this trick it is not the speed of your hand but the smoothness of your actions that matters.

WHAT YOU NEED

A coin

DIFFICULTY RATING: 4

1 Standing to the left of your seated helper, show them a coin. Explain that you will hit your left hand three times with the coin, which will then vanish. As you divulge what will happen, bring the coin down and hit your hand to show the action.

2 Raise your hand above the person's head and bring it down on to your hand, saying 'One'. Repeat this action, saying 'Two'. The third time, raise the coin and leave it on top of your head, positioned so it does not fall.

3 Bring your hand down and say 'Three!' while at the same time opening out both hands and turning them over to show the coin has vanished.

• *When counting before the coin vanishes, always raise your hand to the same spot just above your head. This way, there will be no noticeable change in timing or movement when you place the coin on your head.*

• *Practise placing the coin on your head so you know exactly where to put it.*

• *Practise tilting your head forwards so the coin lands as you count 'Three'. As the coin falls, take a step back and look up so you distance yourself from where the coin has appeared.*

4 The seated person will probably look up at you, but there is nothing to see, as the coin will be out of sight. You can roll your sleeves up and let the person check your hands but the coin is nowhere to be found.

5 To make the coin reappear, get the helper to cup both hands in front of them. Point to their hands, saying they will see the coin return on the count of three.

6 On the count of 'Two' tilt your head forwards so the coin slides off. Time it correctly and the coin will fall into the helper's hands as you get to 'Three'. The coin will seem to appear from nowhere.

Where on Earth...?

THE ILLUSION

After covering a coin with a handkerchief, use your skilled sleight of hand to make it disappear into thin air!

WHAT YOU NEED

A coin
A handkerchief
A shirt with a breast pocket

DIFFICULTY RATING: 2

PRESENTATION

- *It is important that once the coin has been dropped into the pocket, your left hand moves away from it. Do not pause when dropping the coin and practise making a continuous backwards movement with the handkerchief.*

1 Hold the coin by its edge in your right hand. Hold the handkerchief by one corner in your left hand, clipped between your index and your middle fingers.

2 Drape the handkerchief over the coin from the front. As your left hand passes over your right, you secretly take the coin back towards you. Your right fingers remain still while your left hand moves back to your breast pocket, where it drops the coin. The handkerchief conceals this action from the audience.

3 With the handkerchief still covering your right hand, move your left hand away from the breast pocket and continue to drag the handkerchief backwards over your right hand. Your right hand comes in to view and the coin has vanished. Show your audience that both hands are empty and drop the handkerchief on to the table to finish.

Sandwich Secrets

THE ILLUSION

Taking a bread roll off the table, you break it open to find a coin inside.

WHAT YOU NEED

A bread roll
A coin

DIFFICULTY RATING: 2

PRESENTATION

- *Bring the bread roll over to your right hand, rather than bringing your right hand over to the bread roll. In this way, all the attention is on the bread roll, rather than your right hand.*
- *This is a good way to produce the coin that you made disappear in Where Did the Money Go? (see page 76).*

1 Hold the coin in your right hand at the base of your middle two fingers. Keep all your fingers curled slightly in a natural position. With your left hand, pick up the roll with your thumb on top and fingers underneath. Bring your two hands together, placing the roll on top of the coin and letting it slip down to your fingertips.

2 Break the bread roll by pushing up with your fingers while simultaneously moving your thumbs apart, tearing open the roll. Use your fingers to push the coin into the bread; do not tear the roll from underneath.

3 Keep pushing the coin upwards until it becomes visible inside the roll. From the top, it looks like the coin has been buried inside the bread roll. Once the coin is visible, tear the roll in half to get rid of the hole underneath.

Going... Going...
Gone

THE ILLUSION

You tap a coin with a pen, and on the third tap the pen vanishes. Then you find the pen, but the coin disappears. There is quite a bit to learn with this trick as it has several phases. It is also a good trick to practise timing your actions – the smoother you can make them, the more impressive the trick will be.

WHAT YOU NEED

A pen
A coin
Trousers or jacket with
  a pocket

DIFFICULTY RATING: 3

1 Hold the coin parallel to the floor between the index finger and the thumb of your left hand. Take the pen in your other hand. Say 'I will hit the coin with the pen three times. And on the third time it will vanish!'. As you say this, tap the coin with the tip of the pen.

2 Stand with your left side facing the audience. Bring the pen up so it brushes the right side of your head then bring it down to tap the coin. 'One'. Again lift the pen up to the right side of your head then tap the coin. 'Two'.

3 On the third time, bring the pen up to your head, and leave it behind your right ear smoothly. Bring your empty right hand down to the coin. 'THREE!' Look at the coin, turn your hands over and show that the pen has gone.

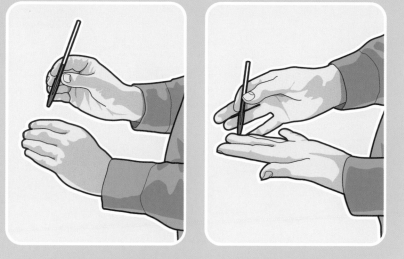

- *When you bring the pen up to the side of your head, always put it behind your ear. In this way, you always perform exactly the same action and, when it is time to leave it there (on the third tap), you will find it a lot easier.*
- *As you tap the coin with the pen, be sure to look at the coin. If you direct your gaze there so will the audience.*

4 To make the coin vanish, turn your body to the left so your right side is facing the audience, revealing the pen. As the audience sees the pen, take it from your ear with your right hand and drop the coin into a left-side pocket from your left hand.

5 Your fingers and thumb still hold the same pose as though the coin was there. Take the pen and say, 'Oh, you want the COIN to vanish?'. Immediately bring the pen down to your left hand, open up the left-hand fingers and thumb and say, 'FOUR!'. The coin has now vanished.

Show Me the Money

THE ILLUSION

As you rub a coin against your sleeve it penetrates your sleeve and ends up inside. If you can make a trick like this one look impromptu when you have, in reality, set it up beforehand, your audience will be incredibly impressed.

WHAT YOU NEED

Two identical coins
A jacket or shirt with long sleeves.

DIFFICULTY RATING: 3

1 Place one of the coins inside your right sleeve and place the other coin in the palm of your right hand at the base of your fingers. Pick it up with your left hand and show it at your fingertips.

2 Bend your right arm and move your right hand up to your neck as though you were resting on your hand. This makes the coin inside your sleeve fall down to your elbow. Rub the other coin against your sleeve at a spot just above your elbow.

3 Allow the coin to drop on to the table. Pick it up with your right hand and hold it at the base of your fingers as before.

4 Place your left-hand fingers over the coin in exactly the same way as when you picked it up last time but now hide it in your right hand as your left hand pretends to take it. This action must look the same as when you really did take the coin.

5 Bend your right arm and move your right hand up to your neck. Rub your left hand against your sleeve as before. While you and the audience watch your left hand, secretly drop the coin down the neck of your shirt.

6 Continue to rub your left hand against your sleeve. Finish with a pressing action, as though you have pushed the coin through your sleeve. Show your audience that your left hand is empty and attract attention to your sleeve and show the outline of a coin inside it.

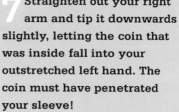

7 Straighten out your right arm and tip it downwards slightly, letting the coin that was inside fall into your outstretched left hand. The coin must have penetrated your sleeve!

The Triple Prediction

THE ILLUSION

After making three predictions about how many cards both you and a helper have, you then go on to show that each prediction is correct. This sneaky trick relies on simple mathematics. However, the routine is presented so that it seems impossible for you to know the information. Simple and straightforward tricks, such as this one, are good to perform because you can concentrate on the presentation without worrying about sleight of hand.

WHAT YOU NEED

A pack of cards
A collection of coins

DIFFICULTY RATING: 2

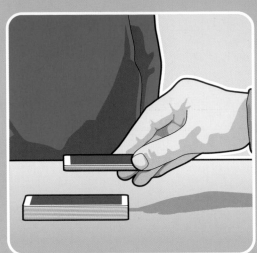

1 Get a helper to shuffle the cards and place them on the table. While your back is turned, get them to pick up a small packet of 10–20 cards. When they do this, ask them to hide the cards under the table so you cannot see them.

2 Turn back round and cut off 25–35 cards. Hide your cards under the table. Ask the helper to silently count how many cards they hold. Do the same with your cards. Let us call your total 'X'. State that you have as many cards as the other person, 3 more and enough to make the person's total up to X – 3. Ask the person to count their cards. You count yours up to this number. Count 3 more, then, starting from the person's total, count the rest of your cards to bring their total up to X – 3 cards.

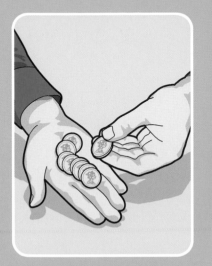

3 You can do the same trick with a bunch of coins. Save up a collection of coins that are all the same value and put them in a bag or box. Get the person to reach inside and remove a handful of coins, and then to add up the amount of money they hold.

4 You make the same prediction as before, but this time, instead of predicting the number of objects, you can predict that you have the same amount of money (X) as the person, a small amount (Y) of money more and enough to make yours up to X – Y. You will always be correct, as long as you take more coins than the other person.

Memorizing With a Difference

THE ILLUSION

A helper chooses a card, looks at and remembers it, then replaces it in a different position. Although the cards were all face down, you know which card has been moved. This trick does require setting up, so it is a great first trick. Sometimes, it is better to present a trick as a show of skill rather than as a piece of magic. You will get credit for skills you do not possess!

WHAT YOU NEED

A pack of cards

DIFFICULTY RATING: 1

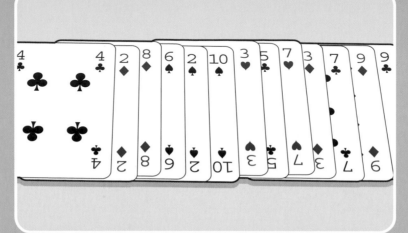

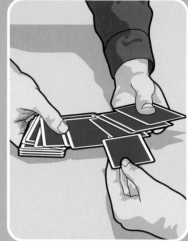

1 Before you start, you must secretly set up the cards. Separate the cards, with all the even-numbered cards and Queens mixed in one pile, and the odd-numbered cards, Jacks and Kings mixed in another pile. Place the pile containing the even numbers and Queens on top of the other pile.

2 Spread the top half of the pack and ask a helper to choose a card from this half. Ask the helper to look at and remember their card. Square the remaining cards neatly.

- *Do not worry if someone wants to choose a card from the bottom half of the pack. Let them do so, but make sure they replace it in the top half, and then go through the cards from the top half.*
- *There are other ways to split the pack into halves. One is to have odd black cards and even red cards on the top with even black cards and odd red cards on the bottom. A clever separation is round versus non-round numbers: 2, 3, 6, 8, 9, 10 and Q all have round tops to them while A, 4, 5, 7, J and K are either flat or pointed on top.*

3 Re-spread the cards, this time using the bottom half of the pack and ask for the selected card to be replaced. Look away as the selected card is replaced somewhere in the bottom half of the pack, then square up the pack in your hand.

4 Go through the pack from the bottom to find the card. You will see all odd cards except for one even card or Queen. This is the card that was replaced in the opposite half. Because you already know the card, you can then reveal it in any way you like.

5 You could simply take the card out and place it on the table. Ask the person to name their card and get them to turn the card over. As you talk, casually shuffle the cards to get rid of any evidence of the order of the cards.

Spot the Thief

THE ILLUSION

Unseen by you, someone in a group of people hides an object on them. You are able to tell who has the hidden object. This trick introduces the idea of a secret assistant. When people think you are doing the trick by yourself, they will be incredulous at what they see, as there is absolutely no explanation for how you could possibly know the right person. Used in the right way, the secret assistant is a useful addition to your magical portfolio but must not be overused.

WHAT YOU NEED

A small object
A secret assistant

DIFFICULTY RATING: 1

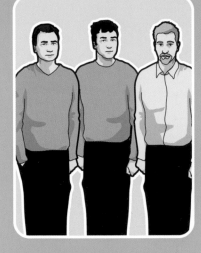

1 Hand a small object to a group of people. When your back is turned, one of them is to take the object and place it in their pocket – your assistant notes who this is. Once this is done, turn back around to face them.

2 To identify who has the object, your assistant simply copies the actions of the person who has the object. If the person's arms are crossed, your assistant crosses their arms too. If their hand is on their chin, your assistant copies them. Your assistant must not make it obvious that they are copying.

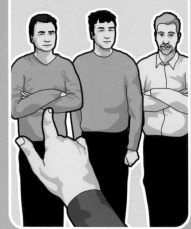

3 Look at your assistant and then check to see who else is in the same position. Once you know, pretend to look at body language, make eye contact or ask questions to make people think you are using psychology to figure out who has the hidden object.

It's Black Magic

THE ILLUSION

While your back is turned or you are out the room, someone selects an object from several on the table. The trick is that you always know which one is selected. This easy-to-learn trick also requires an assistant, and this time the person is helping you with a secret code. Once you and a friend know the secret, you will be able to do this trick at any time.

WHAT YOU NEED

A variety of everyday objects, one of which must be black
A secret assistant

DIFFICULTY RATING: 1

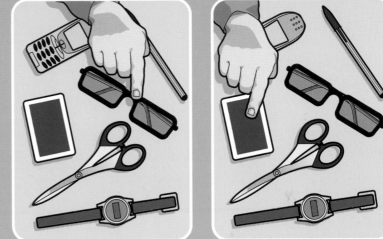

1 Spread out the objects on the table. While your back is turned, someone silently points to one of the objects on the table. Your secret assistant notes which this is.

2 When you turn back, your assistant points to each object. The secret is this: after your assistant points to the black object, the next object pointed to is the chosen one. If the black object is the one chosen, this is pointed to last.

The Secret is the Placement

THE ILLUSION

While you are not looking, someone chooses one of the cards on the table. As elsewhere, your assistant knows the secret code and shows you which is the chosen card. There are two versions: using ten cards or nine cards and the empty cardboard packet for the cards. So, you can always repeat the trick by varying the method. You should never repeat a trick too often, though, or you'll be found out.

WHAT YOU NEED

A pack of cards
A secret assistant

DIFFICULTY RATING: 1

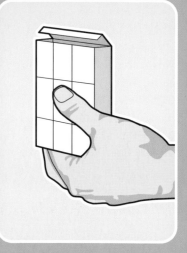

1 To set up the trick take ten cards, one of which must be a ten. Arrange them on the table in two columns of four with two cards in the middle – the identical layout to the spot arrangement on the ten card. Position the ten card at the bottom right. Turn your back, and get a helper to silently choose a card. Your assistant notes which one this is.

2 Turn back and ask your assistant to point to each card in turn. When they point to the ten card, they place their finger on the spot that corresponds to the position of the chosen card. In the example above, the assistant's finger is pointing to the spot that relates to the Four of Diamonds.

3 A variation of this trick is to lay out any nine cards in three rows of three. This time, your assistant holds a card box. The face of the box is split up into nine imaginary sections, corresponding to the layout of the cards. When your assistant places a thumb in the section corresponding to the position of the chosen card, you know which card to name.

Dastardly Dominoes

THE ILLUSION

Ask someone to create a random chain using dominoes as if playing the game. You predict what the two end numbers will be. This self-working trick uses a little-known principle applied to a set of dominoes. Self-working tricks need not look simple, because you can work on the presentation: emphasize how the person could have chosen any type of chain with different end numbers.

WHAT YOU NEED

A set of dominos

DIFFICULTY RATING: 1

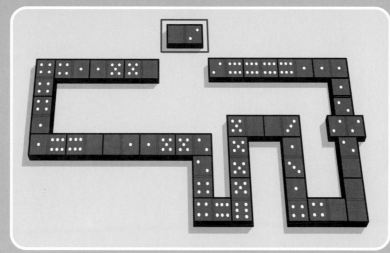

1 Remove any domino from a standard set of dominoes; this domino will form your prediction. Place it in your pocket or anywhere out of sight. Lay out all the remaining dominoes face up on the table. Ask a helper to arrange them in a standard domino chain, with each half of a domino placed next to a matching half from another one. Any domino can be used to start the chain. When the chain is finished, point out the number of spots at the two ends. Bring out your prediction domino to show that the spots on it match those at each end.

PRESENTATION

● *This trick works automatically. Many people do not realize that when laid out in a chain, a set of dominos forms a complete circle. Whichever domino you remove will be the missing link and will be the same as the two ends of any chain formed with the rest of the set.*

Th Ultimat Maths Trick

THE ILLUSION

Using a random set of numbers, you predict a word chosen from a book. This is a well-known mathematical trick among magicians. The process appears to be random but always results in the same total: 1089. This trick is very versatile as you can use the final total in any number of ways.

WHAT YOU NEED

A book
A pen
A piece of paper

DIFFICULTY RATING: 1

BEFORE YOU START

Turn to page 108 in the book. Go to the ninth line down and remember the first word on the line.

1 Hand a helper the pen and paper and tell them to write down any three-digit number, using three different digits between one and nine.

2 Tell the helper to reverse the number and write this new number down underneath the first. Then ask them to subtract the smaller number from the larger one.

NB If this new number contains only 2 digits tell them to add a zero to the beginning.

3 The helper must now reverse this new number and write the reversed number underneath the last total. This time, instruct the helper to combine these two numbers and write down the final total. Only you know that no matter what three-digit number the helper started with, the result will always be the magical 1089.

PRESENTATION

- *Knowing the outcome of the maths before you start allows you to predict any number of things to which 1089 can relate.*
- *Tell the helper to turn to page 10, line 8, and look at the ninth word on the line.*
- *In your pocket, have money adding up to 1,089 units of currency.*
- *Have the number 1089 written as the prediction.*
- *There are many other ways to turn the number 1089 into a prediction. See if you can come up with your own.*

4 Ask the helper how many digits there are in this number. Pretend you don't know the answer so the trick seems more impressive. When they tell you the number has four digits, tell them to take the first three as a separate number.

5 Hand the book to the helper and tell them to turn to the page represented by the first three digits of their number. It will always be page 108. When they find the page, ask them to go down to the line represented by the fourth digit in their number. This will always be the ninth line down.

6 Get the helper to concentrate on the first word on that line. Take the pen and paper back from them and, after pretending to read their mind, write down the word you remembered before you started. Tell the person to name the word they are thinking of and show them that you have written down the very same word.

Prepared for All Eventualities

THE ILLUSION

Someone chooses one of three envelopes and you predict which one is chosen. To account for the three different choices you have to have done some preparation beforehand. There are three variations: what makes the trick so good is that each version does not give a clue to the others. The prediction you reveal seems to be the only one possible, which makes it look all the more impressive.

WHAT YOU NEED

Three small envelopes
Three cards that fit inside the envelopes
A marker pen
A coin

DIFFICULTY RATING: 2

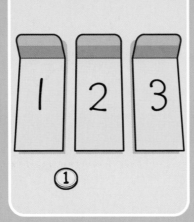

1 Before you start, write a large number 1, 2 and 3 on the back of the envelopes, where the flap is stuck down. Write the number 1 on one side of the coin.

2 On two of the cards, draw large crosses and on the third draw a large tick. Place the card with the tick into envelope number 2 and place each of the other cards into the other envelopes.

3 Now, turn the envelopes over. On the front of envelopes 1 and 2 draw a large cross. On envelope 3, draw a large tick. Turn the envelopes back over so just the numbers are showing. Place the coin on the table with the number side down. Now, you are ready to start.

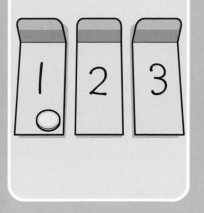

4 Ask a helper to place the coin on one of the envelopes. Depending on which envelope is chosen, the ending is different. If it is envelope 1, tell the helper to turn over the coin, revealing a '1' on its underside.

5 If envelope 2 is chosen, open up envelopes 1 and 3 to show the large crosses. Then, open up envelope 2 to show the tick.

6 If envelope 3 is chosen, turn over envelopes 1 and 2 to show the crosses. Turn over envelope 3 to show the tick. In each case, you knew which envelope was going to be chosen.

PRESENTATION

- *The method of changing the ending depending on what happens during the trick is called an 'out'. The audience does not know what the ending is going to be and so have no idea of the other versions you never used.*

- *Do not hesitate when going to show your prediction. Know where each prediction is for each number so you don't show the wrong one.*

- *When envelopes 2 or 3 are chosen, always show the predictions for the wrong envelopes first. This builds tension for the correct result.*

Pick Any Two, Eliminate One

THE ILLUSION

Items are eliminated from a selection on a table, and you predict which item will be left at the end. Once you learn how this trick works you will be able to employ it in other shows of skill.

WHAT YOU NEED

Six everyday items
A pen
A piece of paper

DIFFICULTY RATING: 2

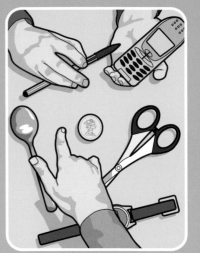

1 Place any six items on the table. These can be anything you like. You are not restricted to six items, but this is a good number to keep the trick short and sweet. You can borrow any or all the items from the helper.

2 Without your helper seeing, secretly draw one of the items on the paper as your prediction and fold it up so it cannot be seen.

3 Pick up two of the items, but not your predicted item and tell the helper to point to one of them. Tell the helper whichever one they point to will be eliminated. Place the one they point to on one side and return the other item to the selection.

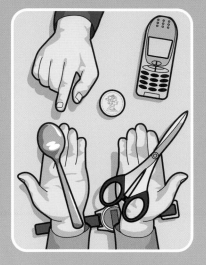

PRESENTATION

- *The simple rule to remember is if there is an even number of items, you must pick up first; if there is an odd number, the helper must pick up first.*
- *While the procedure seems fair, it is obvious that you conspire the circumstances so that your prediction is the last item left. By explaining how you each have a free choice of which item to eliminate, this fact is well hidden.*

4 Tell the person to pick up any two items. If one is the predicted item, choose the other one to be eliminated. If they do not pick up the predicted item, you can eliminate either item.

5 Take turns to pick up two items and have one eliminated. Whenever it is your turn, do not pick up the predicted item; whenever the other person picks up two items, never eliminate the one you've predicted. Continue until there are two items left. One will be the predicted item, so choose the other one. This leaves the predicted item as the last one left.

6 Remind your helper that the choices were random and both of you had the chance to eliminate any item. Show that your prediction matches the item that is left.

The One-handed Cut 1

THE ILLUSION

Cutting the pack with one hand is more of a stunt than a trick. As well as knowing lots of magic tricks, it is always a good idea to intersperse your performance with striking shows of skill. Not only is this cut impressive for your audience, it is also simple to learn and master.

WHAT YOU NEED

A pack of cards

DIFFICULTY RATING: 5

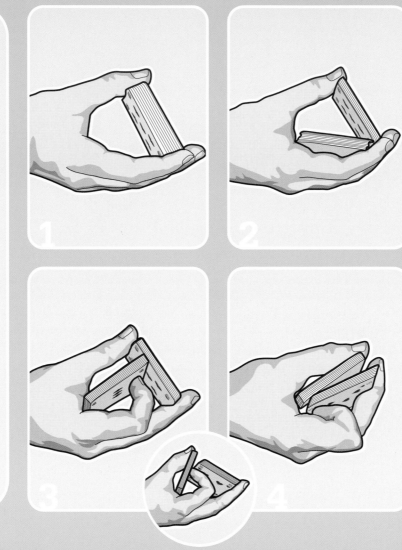

1 Hold the pack in your hand with your palm uppermost. Your fingers are positioned on the bottom long edge and your thumb on the top long edge.

2 Gently release the pressure with your thumb, allowing the bottom half of the pack to fall on to your palm.

3 Bend your index finger underneath this bottom portion with the tip placed near the furthest long edge. Push upwards with your finger and the cards will pivot up. Continue to push until the bottom portion goes past the top portion. Release the top portion with your thumb and allow it to fall on to your index finger.

4 Slowly manoeuvre your index finger to allow the top portion to drop; then lower the bottom portion on top to complete the cut.

Th One-hand d Cut 2

THE ILLUSION
In magic, there is usually more than one way to do something, as well as variations on a theme. This method of cutting the pack with one hand is similar to the the one-handed cut opposite but you may find this version easier. Practise both and see which you prefer or you may find you can do them both.

WHAT YOU NEED
A pack of cards

DIFFICULTY RATING: 5

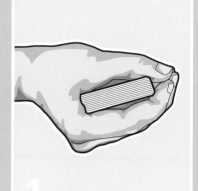

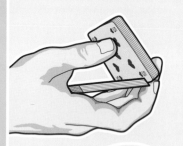

1 Hold the pack deep in the crotch of your thumb. Your thumb and fingertips must be able to reach past the outer long edge of the cards.

2 Lift up about half the pack by the outer edge with your thumb, pivoting it at the crotch of your thumb. At the same time, use your index finger to bend the bottom portion underneath.

3 Extend your index finger upwards, levering the bottom portion up and pivoting it against your fingers. The near long edge will finish above your thumb.

4 Allow the portion held by your thumb to drop on to the palm of your hand, then lower the portion held by your fingers to drop on top to complete the cut.

A Rolling Coin

THE ILLUSION

You roll a coin across the fingers of one hand in another show of skill; this is not as difficult as it looks. You can perform it with coins of any size and it is even possible to do with a finger ring. Try to master it with either hand for maximum wow factor. Plus, it's a great exercise for encouraging the nimble fingers you need for many other tricks.

WHAT YOU NEED

A coin

DIFFICULTY RATING: 5

1 In your right hand hold the coin between your thumb and the side of your index finger, positioned between the knuckle and the first joint. Keep all your fingers bent.

2 Using your thumb, slowly push the coin upwards and on to your index finger. At the same time, lift up your middle finger so the underside is above the coin.

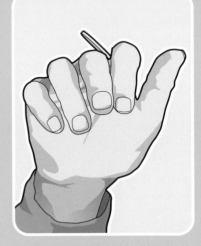

3 Bring your middle finger down so it catches the edge of the coin. Lift up your index finger and the coin will flip on to your middle finger.

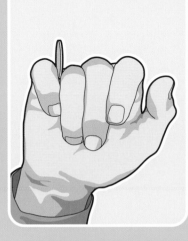

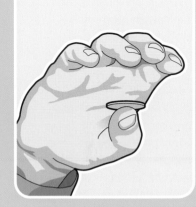

4 Raise your third finger above the coin, then bring it down at the same time as lifting up your middle finger, which makes the coin flip on to your third finger. Lift your fourth finger above the coin.

5 Slowly lower your fourth finger until the coin is clipped upright between it and your third finger.

6 Rotate your hand to the right so that the coin rests on your fourth finger. Bring your thumb across and press the coin against your finger.

7 Rotate your hand back and let go of the coin with your fourth finger so the coin is balanced only on your thumb. Carefully carry the coin under your fingers back to the start position. Repeat as often as you like and practise with different-sized coins.

St␣r Potenti␣l

THE ILLUSION

Use only one hand to form a rubber-band star. While there are several steps to read through, the whole trick takes only about two seconds to perform. This is just one of the many tricks and flourishes that you can do with rubber bands. Mastering skills like this one is great for impromptu gags involving everyday objects. Intersperse your magic tricks with such flourishes to convince your audience that you can do absolutely anything.

WHAT YOU NEED

A rubber band

DIFFICULTY RATING: 3

1 Place the rubber band over your index, third and fourth fingers so it is held at the first joints.

2 Bring your thumb over the strand running between your index finger and your fourth finger then underneath the strand between your third and your fourth fingers.

3 Using the back of your thumb, stretch the strand as you bring your thumb back to its starting position.

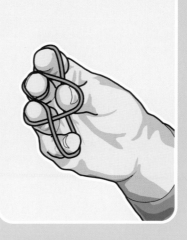

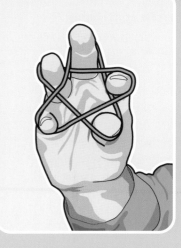

4 Bring your middle finger over the strands then underneath the strand that stretches between your thumb and your little finger.

5 Pull your thumb out of the rubber band while moving your middle finger back to its starting position, pulling back the strand with it.

6 Bring your thumb over the long strand between your index and your little fingers, and then under the strand between your middle and your third fingers.

7 Pull this strand back with your thumb. Open up your fingers: you will have a five-pointed star shape formed in your hand.

Eyes Wide Shut

THE ILLUSION

The level of water in a glass mysteriously falls without you touching it. Some tricks work best when there are only two people involved – you and the person for whom you are performing. Although it is easy to pull the wool over the person's eyes, any onlookers can see how you do it.

WHAT YOU NEED

A glass of water

DIFFICULTY RATING: 3

1 Sit at a table opposite a helper with the glass of water in front of them. Ask your helper to place their hands palms down on either side of the glass.

2 Lean across the table and place an index finger on each arm just below the helper's shoulder.

3 Run your fingers down their arms. Just before you reach their wrists, lift your fingers off a little and place them down on to the backs of their hands.

4 Place your fingers back up to the start position just below the shoulders. Now, before you start, tell your helper to close their eyes.

5 Run your index fingers down their arms as before. Now when you lift them off just before the wrists, extend your right little finger. Take away your left hand and place your right index finger on the back of the helper's right hand with the fourth finger placed on the back of their left hand. The helper will assume they can feel both of your index fingers.

6 With your free left hand, silently pick up the glass and drink some of the water (swallow quietly, too). Then, silently place the glass back on exactly the same spot.

7 Position your left index finger next to the one of your right hand. As you tell the person to open their eyes, curl in your fourth finger and hover your right index finger over their left hand. When the person opens their eyes, they will see both index fingers above their hands, as though they have just been lifted. The water level in the glass has dropped, even though you couldn't pick up the glass.

The Four-coin Roll

THE ILLUSION

Rolling four coins between your fingers is probably the most technically difficult stunt in this book. If you can learn how to do it, you will quite rightly have a huge sense of achievement. What's more, it looks extremely impressive and so is well worth the effort required to master it.

WHAT YOU NEED

Four same-size large coins

DIFFICULTY RATING: 5

1 Hold all four coins in your right hand with your thumb on top and index and middle fingers underneath.

2 Holding the coins between your thumb and your index finger, bend your middle finger upwards and inwards. Bring your third finger across your palm so the coins are resting on it and your index finger. Your little finger now rests just to the left edge of the coins.

3 Slightly tilt your hand to the left and, by gently releasing pressure with your thumb, allow the front two coins to roll to the left while still retaining the grip on the rear two coins. The front two coins now rest on your index and third fingers. The backs of your middle and fourth fingers are on top of the coins. The back of your middle finger also touches the upper edge of the rear two coins.

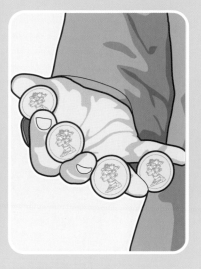

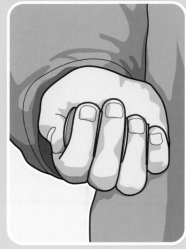

4 Use your thumb to roll the rear coin around your index finger to the right, while your fourth finger starts to roll its front coin around the third finger to the left. Take it slowly and keep your middle finger in contact with the other two coins.

5 Use your thumb and fourth finger to continue to roll their respective coins to the right and left. Start to lower your middle finger, forcing the two middle coins apart.

6 Finish rolling the coins to the sides with your thumb and fourth fingers, and lower your middle finger far enough to clip the middle of the two central coins. All the coins are now displayed, with one coin between each of your fingers and thumb.

7 To finish in style, close all your fingers together, catching the coins so they are held by their faces rather than their edges.

A Glass Act

THE ILLUSION

From underneath a handkerchief you whip out a wine glass. Although the moves are simple to do, there is a lot to learn regarding the timing and gestures. When everything flows together, you can wow your audience with your magical talents.

WHAT YOU NEED

A wine glass
A handkerchief

DIFFICULTY RATING: 4

BEFORE YOU START:

Place the wine glass in your lap with the mouth side down. The base of the wine glass should sit just below the edge of the table.

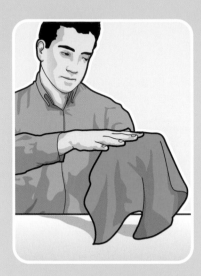

1 Place the handkerchief flat on the palm of your left hand. Tap the handkerchief with your right hand to show there is nothing under it.

2 Stare at the handkerchief and snap the fingers on your right hand. At the same time, bend the fingers of your left hand so that they point upwards. It will look as if something has appeared underneath the handkerchief.

3 Grip the handkerchief by its inner corner in your right hand and slowly pull it off your left hand towards the table edge. Shift your focus to your left hand, to help build the tension. As your right hand reaches the table edge, clip the wine glass stem with your middle and your third fingers. At this point, move your left hand forward to reveal your fingers.

4 When they see your empty left hand the audience relaxes. At this moment, lift the wine glass under the handkerchief above the level of the table using your right hand. Keep the wine glass below your palm-up hand, hidden by the handkerchief, look at your left hand and joke about producing your fingers.

5 Now, bring attention to your right hand, moving it away from the edge of the table. Slightly bend your fingers so the base of the glass does not show. Pat the handkerchief as before to show that there is nothing in your hand.

6 Using your left hand, lift up the middle of the handkerchief and, at the same time, bend your fingers inwards, causing the wine glass to pivot around on to your palm-up hand. Drop the handkerchief; the audience will expect it to fall flat on the table, except this time it doesn't.

7 Grip the wine glass by the stem. Pull the corner of the handkerchief towards you to reveal that the wine glass has magically appeared in your right hand.

A Cracking Time

THE ILLUSION

You bend your finger back and the audience hears a loud cracking noise. This is a simple stunt to perform before you start your routine of tricks. But as it can be very convincing, be sure that no one in the audience is of a nervous disposition!

WHAT YOU NEED

Two hands

DIFFICULTY RATING: 1

1 Hold out your right hand palm uppermost with the fingers apart. Hold your right index finger loosely in the palm of your closed left hand.

2 Twist your left hand forwards, bending your right index finger back a short way. At the same time, snap your left thumb against your left fingers so a cracking sound is heard. Timing these two actions simultaneously makes it look and sound like you cracked your right index finger.

PRESENTATION

- *Practise snapping your fingers and thumb so you can produce a crisp cracking sound each time you do the trick.*
- *This is perfect to do before you start other tricks. Explain that magicians need to limber up and get their hands ready for work. Pretend to crack each finger of your hand by repeating the actions for each one.*
- *You can also crack someone else's finger by gripping it as you would your own – be careful you do not bend it back too far, though.*

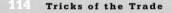

The Unravelling Tie

THE ILLUSION

This amusing trick can be done on the spur of the moment. Whenever someone is wearing a tie, you can try out this stunt and give them a shock! It will bemuse your audience to see a tie apparently being unravelled without any damage actually being done.

WHAT YOU NEED

A helper wearing a tie

DIFFICULTY RATING: 2

1 Stand to the helper's left, turn your right hand palm uppermost and take hold of their tie; your thumb should be on top and your fingers hidden underneath. Appear to find a bit of thread and pick it out from the tip of the tie with your left hand.

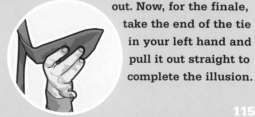

2 Hold the invisible thread in your left hand and pull it out from the tie. At the same time as you pull with your left hand, flick your right middle finger upwards several times, making the tie flap. With your left hand, pretend to pull more thread out, repeating the flapping action.

3 To finish, pretend to get the last bit of thread in your left hand and pull it out. Press your right thumb down against your fingers then, in one quick action, slide it towards the helper. The tie will bunch up, as though the thread has come all the way out. Now, for the finale, take the end of the tie in your left hand and pull it out straight to complete the illusion.

Shrinky Dink Pencil

THE ILLUSION
A pencil appears to shrink to half its size as you hold it in your hands. Practise this trick in front of a mirror, even you will be astounded by this remarkable optical illusion.

WHAT YOU NEED
A pencil

DIFFICULTY RATING: 2

1 Hold the pencil in your right hand at about shoulder height, with your hand out to the side and not underneath the pencil. Hold it right at its end to show as much of the pencil length as possible. This makes the illusion more impressive.

2 Bring your left hand in from the side and position it so about half the pencil is hidden by your left fingers. At the same time that you grasp the pencil with your left hand, let go with your right hand and move it to the right.

3 Bring your right hand in from the side and grasp hold of the pencil so half the length is now hidden by your right fingers. At the same time, let go with the left hand and move it to the left. Repeat grasping and letting go with each hand. By speeding the actions up, the pencil will appear to shrink.

What's the Catch?

THE ILLUSION
Your audience will see and hear your invisible coin land in the paper bag. And you reach in the bag to reveal a coin that has apparently materialized from out of nowhere. So, it seems that you can take advantage of your audience by tricking their eyes or their ears.

WHAT YOU NEED
A large coin
A paper bag
A top with long sleeves

DIFFICULTY RATING: 2

1 Before you start, place the coin in your left sleeve. Hold the bag with your thumb on the outside and your index and middle fingers on the inside. Open the mouth of the bag using your left hand. Pretend to take a coin out of your pocket and flick it up into the air. Look up and follow its apparent path with your eyes.

2 As you watch the invisible coin fall, hold the bag out ready to catch it. As the coin apparently drops into the bag, snap your thumb against your fingers. This move causes the bag to crumple and makes a noise simulating a coin landing in the bag.

3 Time your gaze so you snap your fingers at the same time as you look down to the bag. Reach into the bag with your left hand. As your arm drops down, the coin will fall into your fingers. Make sure your hand is inside the bag before the coin comes into view. Reach into the bottom of the bag and produce the coin.

Simply Spoon Bending

THE ILLUSION

Bending cutlery is a common visual effect used in magic and is a trick that many people will have seen performed on television. It catches people off guard to see a solid spoon bending right before their eyes. And there's no reason to stick solely to spoons; before you know it you could be bending all manner of cutlery.

WHAT YOU NEED

A table spoon

DIFFICULTY RATING: 3

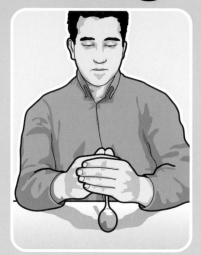

1 Hold the spoon in your right hand, with the tip of the bowl's underside towards the audience and touching the table. Rest your thumb on the end of the handle.

2 Bring your left hand over and rest the fingers on the backs of the fingers of your right hand. When your right fingers are covered, secretly place your right little finger behind the handle above the bowl. Place your left thumb next to your right on the handle. Both thumbs rest on the sides of your index fingers, hiding the handle from view.

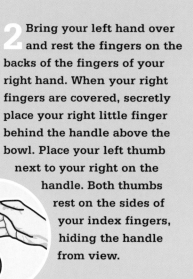

3 Keep the tip of the bowl stationary and bring both hands down towards the table, causing the spoon to pivot downwards against your little finger. Tilt your hands forwards a little as they move downwards. Keep both thumbs against your index fingers, still hiding the handle.

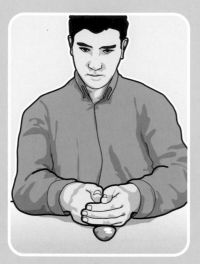

PRESENTATION

- *Practise the moves until they are fluid. Eventually, you will be able to pick up the spoon and immediately go into the correct position for the trick.*
- *Act as if you are really bending the spoon, which would take a lot of effort. Bend it slowly, tensing your face, hand and arm muscles to look as convincing as possible.*

4 Continue to lower your hands, tilting them forwards until your right little finger hits the table. From the front, it appears the spoon is bent. The thumbs still remain on the fingertips, making sure that the gap where the handle should be is not visible.

5 To finish, bring your hands straight up and the spoon will pivot upwards. When it is vertical, slip your left hand down the handle, making sure that your right little finger is still covered.

6 Twist the spoon through 180 degrees by tilting your right hand forwards and moving your left hand upwards and towards you. Move your right little finger to the front of the handle, at the same time clipping it between your left index and middle fingers. Show the audience that the spoon is restored.

Magical Mystery Tour

THE ILLUSION
You place an object such as a used party popper or a thimble under your arm, then make it reappear behind your knee. This fun trick can be performed using almost anything and can be repeated in front of the same person without them seeing how it's done, no matter how many times they watch you.

WHAT YOU NEED
A used party popper or thimble

DIFFICULTY RATING: 3

1 After making sure the party popper is empty, place it on your right thumb. Hold your hand in a fist with your thumb pointing upwards.

2 Place your thumb under your left arm. As it goes out of sight, bend your thumb in, grip the party popper in your curled fingers and remove your thumb, leaving the party popper in place. Hold your arm against your side as though holding the party popper under your arm.

3 Bring your thumb out to show that the party popper is missing. The audience assumes it is under your arm.

4 Move your right hand down to behind your right knee, making sure the party popper is hidden from view by your fingers.

5 While out of sight behind your knee, bend your thumb back into the party popper. Straighten it out then bring your thumb into view, with the party popper sitting on top of it.

6 It will look as though the party popper has travelled from under your left arm to behind your right knee. Hold the party popper in front of you with a 'thumbs-up' pose to finish.

The Coin–Card Sandwich

THE ILLUSION

You have two playing cards and show your audience both sides. Then put the cards together, rub them and, magically, a coin appears. This is another trick often used by professional magicians. It proves that it is not necessarily the speed of the hand that fools the eyes. This trick is best done slowly and smoothly. As no one expects to see the coin at the end, there is no need to worry about people seeing it before you produce it.

WHAT YOU NEED

Two playing cards
A coin

DIFFICULTY RATING: 3

1 Before you start, place the coin in your right hand and hold it near the fingertips. Place one card in your right hand, covering the coin and pick up the other card in your left hand. Hold both cards face down at their corners with your fingers slightly curled.

2 Show the faces of both cards to the audience by tilting them up towards you. As the faces come into view, use your thumbs to push the cards forwards until they are held at the tips of your fingers. The coin stays in place; your fingers hide it from view at the front.

3 Lower both cards and use your thumbs to pull them back again. Place the left-hand card on the right one so it overlaps a little. As soon as the cards overlap, slide the coin across, transfer the grip to the fingers of your left hand and hold the coin against the face of the left-hand card.

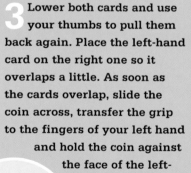

4 Turn the right-hand card face up by placing your middle finger on top and flipping it over between your middle and your index fingers. Repeat the actions of overlapping the cards, this time sliding the coin across to the right and holding it against the face of the right-hand card.

5 Turn the left-hand card face up in the same way as you did for the right-hand card. Both cards are now face up, and the audience has seen the front and the back of each card. The coin is hidden beneath the right-hand card, resting on your fingers.

6 Place the left-hand card underneath the right one so it extends about 2.5 cm (1 in) further forwards. The coin will be sandwiched between the two cards. Tilt the cards down a little and rub them together, so the coin slowly slides forwards.

7 The coin will eventually appear from between the two cards. Hold your left hand out palm uppermost and let the coin drop into it. The appearance of the coin will be a big surprise to the audience.

Candle in the Wind

THE ILLUSION
You extinguish a candle by blowing through a solid wine bottle. But how? Magic does not just rely on the skill of the magician, sometimes the laws of physics are there to help you as well.

WHAT YOU NEED
A candle
A wine bottle

DIFFICULTY RATING: 1

1 Light the candle and hold it in your right hand. Hold the bottle in your left hand between your face and the candle. Each of the trio should be about 10 cm (4 in) away from the other.

2 Blow hard towards the bottle and the candle will be extinguished. The air you blow goes around the bottle and carries on behind it.

PRESENTATION
- *Experiment to see how close the candle needs to be to the bottle so that you are still able to extinguish it. Also see how far away you can be and how hard you need to blow.*
- *This is a fun way to blow out a candle at the end of a dinner party. If the candle is low enough, place the bottle on the table in front of it, bend down and blow out the candle through the bottle.*
- *Always be careful when using lit candles.*

Apple Bobbing

THE ILLUSION

You throw an apple on the floor and it bounces back up. Everyone knows that apples don't bounce – but with the combination of seeing something happen as well as hearing it, the audience will find it difficult to disbelieve. When you have mastered the actions and timing, you can perform this trick using any object that is small enough to hold in your hand.

WHAT YOU NEED

An apple or any round fruit

DIFFICULTY RATING: 3

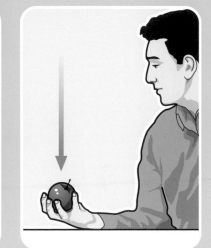

1 Seated behind a table, pick up the apple and turn to the right. Lower your hand as though throwing the apple on the floor. Look down to indicate where you will 'throw' the apple.

2 Just as your hand gets to its lowest point, lift your right foot and loudly tap it back down. At the same time, turn your hand palm up and flick your wrist upwards, throwing the apple into the air. Keep your hand below the table top.

3 Your right hand has remained under the table as the apple is thrown into the air. Now bring it above the table to catch the apple. It appears to the audience as though the apple bounced on the floor and you caught it.

Index

Acknowledgements

I would like to thank all the magicians who have helped shape me and my approach to magic. Some are well aware of their influence while others do not realize that I owe them a debt of gratitude. Through them I have learned much about this wonderful world of magic and now I am able to pass on some of my knowledge to you, the reader.

Thank you to everyone at Hamlyn for bringing this book out from inside my head and onto paper. I would like to thank my parents for helping me to realize my ambition of being a professional magician. Thank you, Vanuatu. Above all, I dedicate this book to my wife Melanie and my son Zachary. They bring so much happiness and laughter into my life and I love them both more than anything in the world.

Commissioning editor: Trevor Davies
Editor: Alice Tyler

Executive art editor: Geoff Fennell
Designer: Barbara Zuniga

Illustrator: Sudden Impact Media
Production controller: Martin Croshaw